What They Didn't Teach You in Graduate School 3.0

This updated edition of a beloved classic explores the often unspoken nuances of life in and beyond graduate school. With new hints that give a 360-degree review of the challenges and issues in academic life, Drew, Feldman, and Gray provide a straightforward, entertaining perspective on matters that affect careers and livelihood. Topics span the dissertation process, job hunting, life in the classroom, and more—making for the perfect graduate student companion. *What They Didn't Teach You in Graduate School 3.0* is an irreverent, one-of-a-kind guide for both graduate students and junior professors as they begin carving their paths toward a successful academic career.

David E. Drew holds the Joseph B. Platt Chair at the Claremont Graduate University (CGU), CA, USA, and previously served as Dean of the CGU School of Educational Studies.

Sue S. Feldman is a Professor and Director of Graduate Programs in Health Informatics at the University of Alabama at Birmingham (UAB), USA.

Paul Gray was Professor of Information Science at the Claremont Graduate University (CGU), CA, USA, and was the Founder of the CGU programs in Information Systems.

PRAISE FOR THE PREVIOUS EDITIONS

"Filled with enough advice to help keep one engaged and productive for an entire academic career."

The Journal of Scholarly Publishing

"We plan to buy one of these for each of our incoming faculty and doctoral students. Take a look. It's a wonderful read."

Dennis E. Gregory, *The Review of Higher Education*

"A voice of wisdom from veteran professors . . . This book is your roadmap . . . I found myself reading this book at least twice a year for the next decade."

Ryan Nivens, *Professor of Mathematics Education, East Tennessee State University, USA*

What They Didn't Teach You in Graduate School 3.0

360 Helpful Hints for Success in Your Academic Career

Third Edition

David E. Drew,
Sue S. Feldman,
and Paul Gray

NEW YORK AND LONDON

Cover Art © 2011 and 2024 by Matthew Henry Hall
Cartoons © 2008, 2011, 2024 by Matthew Henry Hall

Third edition published 2025
by Routledge
605 Third Avenue, New York, NY 10158

and by Routledge
4 Park Square, Milton Park, Abingdon, Oxon, OX14 4RN

Routledge is an imprint of the Taylor & Francis Group, an informa business

© 2025 Taylor & Francis

The right of David E. Drew and Sue S. Feldman to be identified as authors of this work has been asserted in accordance with sections 77 and 78 of the Copyright, Designs and Patents Act 1988.

All rights reserved. No part of this book may be reprinted or reproduced or utilised in any form or by any electronic, mechanical, or other means, now known or hereafter invented, including photocopying and recording, or in any information storage or retrieval system, without permission in writing from the publishers.

Trademark notice: Product or corporate names may be trademarks or registered trademarks and are used only for identification and explanation without intent to infringe.

First edition published by Stylus 2008
Second edition published by Routledge 2012

Library of Congress Cataloging-in-Publication Data
Names: Drew, David E., author. | Feldman, Sue S., author. | Gray, Paul, 1930–2012, author.
Title: What they didn't teach you in graduate school 3.0 : 360 helpful hints for success in your academic career / David E. Drew, Sue S. Feldman, and Paul Gray.
Description: Third edition. | New York, NY : Routledge, 2025. | Previous edition published in 2012. | Includes bibliographical references.
Identifiers: LCCN 2024032578 (print) | LCCN 2024032579 (ebook) | ISBN 9781032581453 (hardback) | ISBN 9781032581729 (paperback) | ISBN 9781003448686 (ebook)
Subjects: LCSH: College teaching—Vocational guidance—United States. | College teachers—United States. | First year teachers—United States.
Classification: LCC LB1778.2 .G73 2025 (print) | LCC LB1778.2 (ebook) | DDC 378.1/202373—dc23/eng/20240928
LC record available at https://lccn.loc.gov/2024032578
LC ebook record available at https://lccn.loc.gov/2024032579

ISBN: 978-1-032-58145-3 (hbk)
ISBN: 978-1-032-58172-9 (pbk)
ISBN: 978-1-003-44868-6 (ebk)

DOI: 10.4324/9781003448686

Typeset in Perpetua
by Apex CoVantage, LLC

To the memory of Paul and Muriel Gray

Contents

A Note About the Authors — xxviii
Acknowledgments — xxx
Foreword by Ryan Nivens — xxxi

Introduction — 1

CHAPTER 1
Basic Concepts — 5

1. Gray's Theorem $N + 2$ — 7
2. Most academic fields are dominated by fewer than 100 powerful people — 7
3. How to become known — 7
4. Drew's Law on publishing papers — 7
5. Make sure you have at least one mentor early in your career — 7
6. Feldman's Rule of Mentoring — 7
7. Specialize—get known for *something*. It helps visibility — 8
8. Trust (yourself and others) — 8

9	Always treat people with respect	8
10	Above all, try also to have fun	8

CHAPTER 2
The PhD 9

11	Job preparation	11
12	Cobble together your own mentors inside and outside your department	11
13	Keep your class notes and books	11
14	Finish your PhD as early as possible while gaining the most experience that you can within the safety net of graduate school	11
15	You are never too old and it is never too late	11
16	Be humble about your PhD	11
17	Maybe you *are* a teacher	11
18	A PhD is primarily an indication of survivorship and perseverance	12
19	Avoid using the term "ABD" to refer to yourself	12
20	A PhD is a certification of independent research ability based on a sample of one	12
21	A PhD is a license to reproduce	12
22	You must have the PhD in hand before you can move up the academic ladder	13
23	Anticipate the key danger point in your PhD studies	13
24	The PhD and part-time study	13
25	Avoid Watson's Syndrome	14
26	Celebrate your PhD	14

CHAPTER 3
The Dissertation   15

27	Selecting the dissertation advisory committee	17
28	Let your chair help you identify other committee members	17
29	Prelims/Qualifying exam	17
30	Format of the prelims	18
31	Determine the best time for you to take prelims	18
32	3-paper versus traditional dissertation	18
33	Primary versus secondary data—what you should know	18
34	Finding a dissertation topic is not as easy as it looks	19
35	Problem-solving mode	19
36	Review a published dissertation	20
37	Put a lot of effort into writing your dissertation proposal	20
38	There are always limitations	20
39	Your positionality statement	21
40	The proposed timeline	21
41	The range of your literature review	21
42	The dissertation abstract	21
43	Your concluding paragraphs	21
44	How long is too long for your dissertation? How short is too short?	22
45	The chain of references is vital in doing a literature search	22

46	Match the literature search to the discussion of results and the conclusions	22
47	The risk of results that are not significant	22
48	The dissertation defense	23

CHAPTER 4
Job Hunting — 25

49	Job hunting is a research project	27
50	Pick a place where you and your family want to live that matches your lifestyle	27
51	When to apply for a faculty position	27
52	Find the best possible school for your first job	27
53	Change your field or move every seven years if you really want a broader challenge	27
54	Not-for-profit or for-profit for your first or second job?	28
55	Exceptions to the previous hint	28
56	Prepare your CV carefully	29
57	Dual careers	29
58	The short list	30
59	The campus visit	30
60	Tactics for interviewing	30
61	Dressing for the job interview	31
62	Wardrobe color	31
63	Don't be intimidated by the schools your interviewers attended	31

64	Be discriminating	31
65	Who is interviewing whom?	32
66	Dealing with interviewers who have published less than you have	32
67	Prepare an elevator speech	32
68	You want information about your availability to reach employers you haven't yet considered	33
69	The law of supply and demand applies to academia as much as to other fields	33
70	The assistant dean strategy	33
71	Evaluate a postdoc carefully, particularly if you are in the sciences	34
72	Non-academic opportunities	34
73	Non-university research organizations offer the challenge of research without the need or the opportunity to teach	35
74	Research versus teaching-oriented institutions	35
75	The jobs may be at for-profit institutions	36
76	New programs	36
77	National rankings	36
78	Teaching in a community college	37
79	Online universities	38
80	Teaching overseas for fun and profit	38
81	Determine the culture	39
82	Assessing culture	39

CONTENTS

83	Listen and integrate	39
84	Gather salary and tenure data	40
85	Obtaining information on tenure decisions is tricky	40
86	Ask about the retirement system	40
87	Parking	40
88	Determine "real pay"	42
89	Get the offer in writing, read it, and negotiate before you accept	42
90	Get your PhD before you start the tenure track, unless you are starving or homeless	43
91	Avoid taking your first job at a school you attended	43
92	Choosing among offers	43
93	Positioning yourself for the next job	44
94	If you become unemployed	45

CHAPTER 5
Teaching and Service   47

95	Publications are the only form of portable wealth	49
96	Many colleges and universities value teaching	49
97	Teaching is a learned art	49
98	Be a mentor	49
99	Relationships with students	50
100	Be relatable	50
101	Go to Toastmasters International	50

102	Meeting classes is paramount	50
103	Academia and campus safety	50
104	Consider costs to students when selecting textbooks	51
105	Avoid serving on a committee where you are the technical expert	51
106	Summaries lock in the material	51
107	Encourage questions	51
108	Enjoy your classes	52
109	Lecturing versus facilitating	52
110	Teaching is not synonymous with lecturing	52
111	Flipping the learning	52
112	Lecture capture	53
113	Presentation software	53
114	Digital natives versus digital immigrants	54
115	Distance education	54
116	Distance learning is a blessing and a threat	55
117	Be wary of student excuses	55
118	Believe it or not, cheating is widespread at some institutions	55
119	Teach every student	55
120	Teach to the student's frame of reference	55
121	Distracted students	56
122	Undergraduates don't recall much from seven or more years ago	56

CONTENTS

123	Will this be on the final?	56
124	Grade inflation	57
125	Keep up with technobabble	57
126	Wikipedia and other Web sources	57
127	Letters of reference for students	58
128	The student as customer mantra	58
129	Be student focused	59
130	FERPA (Family Educational Rights and Privacy Act)	59

CHAPTER 6
Research   61

131	If you want a research career, make sure the position you are offered allows you to actually do research	63
132	You can trade off teaching loads and research opportunities	63
133	Research requires quantitative and qualitative skills, each of which provides different kinds of insights	64
134	Learn grantsmanship; it is a skill like any other	64
135	Don't be modest when writing a grant proposal	64
136	Proposal budgets	64
137	Protest if your brilliant grant proposal is declined	65
138	Build an advisory panel of nationally respected experts in your grant proposal	65
139	If you didn't build in an advisory panel, it's not too late	65
140	Get the grant approval in writing	65

141	Get clearance before you study an organization	65
142	Which brings us to the IRB	66
143	Academic trade journals are sources of higher education (and job) information	67
144	Collaborate and cooperate	67
145	Plagiarism is forbidden	67
146	Generative AI	68
147	Back up, back up, back up your research (actually everything!)	68
148	Many who earn a PhD never publish anything beyond their dissertation; others publish only one article from the dissertation	68

CHAPTER 7
On Writing — 71

149	Learn how to write clearly	73
150	Learn the fine points of English	73
151	Be sure to spell-check, grammar-check, and fact-check your work	73
152	Editing your own material	73
153	Limits on self-plagiarism	74
154	Citations	74
155	More on citations	76
156	Develop a pool of research references stored in your computer	76
157	Reuse the literature search from your dissertation	76
158	Deadlines	77

CHAPTER 8
On Publishing — 79

159 Submit your best articles to the best journals in the field — 81

160 Keep track of your submissions — 81

161 Write most of your articles for refereed journals — 81

162 Avoid writing introductory textbooks if you are not tenured — 81

163 Recognize the difference between writing the first paper on a subject and writing the nth one — 82

164 Writing the nth paper means that $n-1$ papers on the subject were written before yours — 82

165 When writing the nth paper, make sure your contribution to the issue is clear — 82

166 Revise papers quickly — 82

167 Turn around your reviews of other people's papers quickly — 82

168 Publish early and often — 82

169 Your dissertation is a publishing asset — 83

170 The literature search you performed for your dissertation is a treasure trove of information — 83

171 Include single-author papers in your portfolio — 83

172 Co-authoring a paper with a superstar — 83

173 Be aware of delays in publishing — 83

174 Rewards for academic publishing — 84

175 Don't become an editor too early — 85

176 Do serve as a reviewer for journals, particularly top journals — 85

177	Pay attention to the book publishers' representatives who contact you	85
178	Selecting a publisher involves trade-offs	86
179	Get to know the major editors of the book publishers in your field	86

CHAPTER 9
Tenure — 87

180	Tenure is the prize	89
181	Your promotion dossier	89
182	Start your tenure dossier on your first day of employment	90
183	Why tenure is such a hurdle	90
184	Once you achieve tenure, never take another appointment without it	90
185	Tenure, like research support (Hint 184), can be negotiated on the way in	90
186	Tenure is tougher to obtain in cross-disciplinary fields	90
187	Once you achieve tenure, don't stop working	91
188	Once you achieve tenure, don't stop learning	91
189	Tenure is forever (almost)	91
190	Tenure as we know it today may not be here forever	92
191	The number of tenured slots may decrease with time	92
192	Know the tenure clock	92
193	The dreaded impact factor	93
194	Open access vs. closed access	93

CONTENTS

195	Impact factor turned upside down	94
196	Tenure committees look almost exclusively at refereed publications that appear in peer-reviewed journals or in scholarly books	94
197	Downloads count	94
198	Multiple-author papers	95
199	What are key citations indices? Are they important?	95
200	Boosting your index	95
201	Publication quality counts	96
202	Rolling reviews	96

CHAPTER 10
Academic Rank 99

203	Being a tenured full professor is as close to freedom as you can come in US society	101
204	As a full professor, you must be known for something and, in some institutions, that reach must be international	101
205	Avoid becoming the pitied Permanent Associate Professor	101
206	Promotion is a unique opportunity for a larger pay raise	102

CHAPTER 11
Your Financial Life as an Academic 103

207	Academics are risk averse	105
208	Contracts are given to faculty for nine, ten, or twelve months	105
209	Salaries vary by field and by region	105
210	Summer pay	105

211	The zero-raise years	106
212	Retirement savings	106
213	Tax deferral	107
214	Administrators make more	108

CHAPTER 12
Life as an Academic — 109

215	On becoming a dean	111
216	Be prepared to spend time on seemingly petty issues	111
217	Sometimes major administrative decisions are made in informal quick conversations	111
218	Publishing while "deaning"	111
219	Good deans/Bad deans	112
220	Never, ever choose sides in department politics	112
221	Don't accept a joint appointment, particularly as your initial appointment	112
222	Join the faculty club if your school has one	112
223	Office hours	112
224	Online programs	112
225	Sabbaticals	113
226	Maintain collegiality	113
227	As an academic you are a public person	114
228	On recognizing online students	114

CONTENTS

229	Freedom of speech	114
230	Freedom of speech—online	114
231	Attend invited lectures	115
232	Serving as an external reviewer	115
233	Keeping up with your field	116
234	Board of trustees	117
235	Secretaries/administrative assistants are a valuable and scarce resource, and you should treat them as such	117
236	Value your teaching assistants and graders	118
237	Grading	118
238	Your research assistants require supervision	118
239	Physical plant/Facilities	118
240	Be careful what you delegate	119
241	Business cards	119
242	Keeping all things digital in good working order	119
243	Learn the idiosyncrasies of your institution's computer center/IT shop	119
244	Electronic mail (email)	120
245	Phishing	121
246	Don't get on too many email lists	121
247	One last note on email	121
248	Productivity software	121

249	Keep up with digital developments	122
250	Meetings and digital publications	123
251	Interlibrary loans are quicker and more efficient than they used to be	123
252	Use digital libraries if they are available in your field	123
253	The "ungettable" article	124
254	Telecommuting/Work from home (or elsewhere)	124
255	Your website	124
256	Your digital visibility	125
257	What is ORCID and why do I need it?	126
258	Build your brand	126
259	Persistence of language	126
260	Institutional citizen	127
261	Get to know the development people in your school and support them	127
262	Be responsive to the alumni office just as you are to the development office	127
263	When you do something noteworthy, let your school's public relations department know, and ask the staff to publicize it	127
264	Communicating your field to the public	128
265	The Faculty Senate in most institutions provides a forum	128
266	Service	128

267	Never, never become a department chair, even an acting department chair, unless you are a tenured full professor	129
268	Be aware that the powers of a department chair are few	129
269	The role of conflict in the job	129
270	Leadership	130
271	Dealing with student problems	130
272	The redeeming social value of being chair	130
273	Don't stay in the chair position too long	130
274	You can go home again—retreat rights	131
275	Professional travel	131
276	Attend conferences	132
277	Choosing your conferences	132
278	Your conference presentation	133
279	Protect your intellectual capital while traveling	133
280	Working while conferencing	133
281	Drew's rule of conference redundancy	133
282	You may be involved in a student grievance at some point in your academic career	134
283	Faculty grievances	134
284	Sexual harassment	134
285	Faculty rarely volunteer to serve on the grievance committee	135
286	You may become the grievant against your institution	135

287 Myth 1: Faculty enjoy lots of free time 135

288 Myth 2: Faculty's political leanings 135

CHAPTER 13
Equity and Values **137**

289 The continuing goal 140

290 Variations among institutions 140

291 Aligning values 140

292 Assessing colleagues and deans 140

293 Accommodations for students 141

294 Accommodations for you 141

CHAPTER 14
Personal Considerations **143**

295 Learn new things over time 145

296 Sequential careers 145

297 Being an expert witness 146

298 Whistle-blowing 146

299 Don't be a penny-ante thief 147

300 Learn time management 147

301 The meaning of your work will change over time 147

302 Completion time 148

303 Failure is an opportunity 148

CONTENTS

CHAPTER 15
Your Health — 151

304 Mental and physical wellness — 153

305 Avoid stress — 153

306 Breaks — 154

307 Start a health and fitness program if you are not already involved in one — 154

308 Exercise — 154

309 Daily gratitude journaling — 155

310 Addictions — 155

311 Drink water — 155

312 Learning about nutrition — 156

313 Benefits of good nutrition — 156

314 Sleep — 156

315 Who's in charge? — 157

316 Meditation — 157

317 Acupuncture — 157

318 Physical appearance — 157

319 Health and life insurance — 158

CHAPTER 16
Final Thoughts — 161

320 Work smarter, not harder — 163

321 The saying "The rich get richer" holds true in academia as well as in society in general — 163

322 Treat students as though they were guests in your home — 163

APPENDICES — 167
APPENDIX A
Mechanics of the Dissertation — 169

323 Oral examinations in the PhD process can occur in at least three points — 169

324 Visual aids in oral presentations — 170

325 Waiting for the committee's decision after the oral examination — 170

326 Post-oral exam rewrites — 170

327 Faculty signatures — 171

328 External examiners — 172

329 Guests at your dissertation defense — 172

330 Submitting your dissertation to the registrar — 172

APPENDIX B
Outside Income — 173

331 Consulting as a hired hand — 173

332 Don't live on your consulting income — 173

333	Consulting income is taxable	174
334	Grants and contracts	174
335	The summer teaching option	174
336	Regular income versus Schedule C income	174
337	Pro bono work	174
338	Consulting pay rate	175
339	Warning! Teaching elsewhere may be a conflict of interest	175

APPENDIX C
How to Become a Millionaire — 176

340	Making (or not making) a fortune through publishing and public appearances	176
341	Write a best-selling novel	177
342	Use a pseudonym for non-academic publications	177
343	Start your own consulting firm	178
344	Write a college textbook	178
345	Write a textbook for K-12 education	178
346	Write a crossover book	178
347	Save by using a TIAA or other annuity plan	179

APPENDIX D
Writing Hints — 180

348	Explain only what the reader needs to know	180
349	Avoid passive voice, which is dull and pedantic	180

350	Avoid "should" and "must"	181
351	Pay attention to fonts	181
352	You can rarely be *effective and efficient*	181
353	Avoid generalizing from a single case	181
354	Don't be afraid to use numbered or bulleted lists	181
355	Use figures and tables	182
356	Learn to use styles in word processing programs	182
357	Use the spell-checker	182
358	Pay special attention to references	182
359	Eliminate poor writing habits	183
360	Bad words refers to words that cause the reader difficulty rather than words banned by the Federal Communications Commission	183

A Note About the Authors

This book began as the result of a casual lunch conversation years ago between David Drew and Paul Gray. They discovered that each recently had given advice to junior professors about how to survive and succeed in the academic world. They decided to combine their ideas into a memo, which contained about 15 hints. From time to time each would add a hint or two to the memo, which they would hand to junior colleagues. Many years later, as the memo grew, it occurred to them that this possibly could become a book. That book was published by Stylus Press in 2008 and a second edition was published in 2012.

We are sad to report that Paul passed away in 2012, as the result of an automobile accident (that was the fault of the other driver).

Paul Gray was the founder of the programs in Information Systems at the Claremont Graduate University (CGU). Paul was a rare individual whose work reflected both his technology skills and his deep appreciation of language, the arts, and the humanities. He was a pioneer in the development and application of information science; but he also had worked full-time as a professional editor for many years. At any given time, he might be conducting research on health care information systems, advising a symphony orchestra, and editing a professional journal. He was the recipient of many international awards and citations, including the prestigious Lyons Electronic Office (LEO) award of the Association for Information Systems. Furthermore, he was deeply committed to teaching and mentoring, as generations of CGU graduates will attest. He retired in 2001 and continued to teach, conduct research, write, consult, and curate the Paul Gray PC Museum at CGU.

For the third edition of this book, David has been joined by Sue Feldman, who earned an Interfield PhD degree at CGU in both Education and Information Systems and Technology. She, too, has worked across boundaries in several professional fields and presently is a full professor at the University of Alabama at Birmingham (UAB) with appointments in the School of Health Professions and the School of Medicine. She is the Director of Graduate Programs in Health

Informatics and conducts local, national, and international research on information systems for social good and social protections. At UAB, she was honored with the Mentor of the Year award and brings many of those hints to you in this third edition.

A sociologist, David Drew holds the Platt Chair in the Management of Technology and is Professor of Education at CGU. For ten years, he served as dean of the School of Educational Studies. His first career was as a computer scientist; he served as head applications programmer at a leading research university and as a senior information scientist at the Rand Corporation. David has published research about K-12 education, higher education, health care, and technology. However, for many years the highest priorities in his work have been teaching and mentoring.

So, grab your favorite beverage, sit down with this book, and have a "chat" with the authors.

Acknowledgments

The authors and Taylor and Francis Publishing acknowledge *Inside Higher Ed* and a number of doctoral seminars for providing forums for presenting a number of the hints that appeared in the first edition. Articles in *Inside Higher Ed* by Rob Weir, Eliza Wolf, Thomas Wright, and others inspired several hints in the second edition.

Early on, we posted a survey on social media calling for new hints for this third edition. The authors thank everyone who suggested or provided hints for the first two editions and for this third edition: Ashleigh Allgood, Rochelle Altman, Stephen Bronsburg, Maria Cervone, Jana Craft, Thomas English, Anwen Eslinger, Sharon Geaghan, Steven Gump, Danelle Hill, Laura Kazan, Suzie Kovacs, Thomas Luschei, Ryan Nivens, Amough Ananda Rao, Sarah Robertson, Jack Schuster, Akanksha Singh, and Alexis Symons.

Foreword

One of the best and most unrestricted careers in the world is that of professor. As one ventures past the graduation mark of a Bachelor of Art or Science, the number of people who walk with you becomes a smaller and smaller percentage of the population. According to the US Census Bureau, there were approximately 225 million adults over 25 living in the United States in 2021. That year, 10.7 percent of the population had a master's degree, 1.5 percent held a professional degree, and 2.1 percent held a doctorate degree. For those people entering the professoriate, you are joining the ranks of the population that would pass significance at $p < 0.05$ if a person in this group was chosen at random!

Particularly within the United States, the role of a full professor is the last bastion of free-thinking and freedom to dream, think, and create. Many of the technologies we enjoy today are running on a mathematical language of logic that was developed in the 1800s by mathematicians whose job it was to think of ideas regardless of the immediate application. Creative works, inventions, and teaching others how to think—rather than what to think—are the world that a professor inhabits. How exactly one becomes a professor, finds a job as a professor, and thrives and prospers in that role is not always a clearly marked road. In fact, moving beyond a tertiary degree is, in many ways, "beyond the pale," to use a historian's term.

Fortunately, this book is now in its third edition. The story of my career path may or may not match yours, but in the spirit of how the authors wrote this book, I'll finish the balance of this forward with my personal experience—how this book affected me and the eventual success of my career.

I began my career teaching high school mathematics and computer science, and my wife and I had started our family and had two children. In 2008, I took my first job as a faculty member. I had just spent four years in residence with the National Science Foundation (NSF)-funded Center for the Study of Mathematics Curriculum, but I was still "ABD" and needed to get my career moving—and

FOREWORD

support this growing family. To anyone looking from the outside, the odds were stacked against success in academia.

And so, I arrived in July, teaching a summer course for my new university at the *adjunct rate* and began my first semester as assistant professor in August. My department chair had a bag of goodies to welcome me—among which was a copy of the book entitled *What They Didn't Teach You in Graduate School*. I felt more prepared by my doctoral program than many of the other new hires I knew, yet I still took time to check out this book. "Perhaps I'll find an item or two to help me out," I thought to myself. I quickly realized that there was more than just one or two pieces of advice in there, and soon *I found myself reading this book at least twice a year for the next decade*.

It was clear to me that *What They Didn't Teach You in Graduate School* was a voice of wisdom from veteran professors, and in 2014, I was promoted to associate professor and granted tenure. Even then, I continued my bi-annual reading of the book and continued to make decisions based on the words and advice of authors I had never met. Five years later I was promoted to full professor and found myself as free as a person can be in the modern world.

In your role as an academic, you will have a variety of experiences. For most, in your early career you will teach hundreds of undergraduate and graduate students. Some engage in the delivery of professional development to hundreds of classroom teachers. After a few years, you might find yourself being a mentor to junior faculty. At some point, you may delve into publishing your first textbook. And there are other events you may witness, for instance, the firing of a faculty member due to blatant plagiarism, which I would hope you never encounter. There are other aspects of the professoriate that you may be unaware of as a new, or even a seasoned, faculty member. What are the implications and expectations of serving on Faculty Senate or committees rewriting by-laws? Along the way, having a book as your career guide for what to do, what decisions to make, and, overall, how to conduct yourself in all things related to the professoriate is quite helpful. What you will find in this book will guard and protect you from walking blindly into or accepting the various roles you may be presented with as a professor.

While you may or may not take all of the advice in this book (for instance, I recently resigned the role of editor of a newsletter that was struggling before I took it at the start of my career and edited it for 15 years), you will find in this book the advice and guidance you need to succeed regardless of the avenue you take. Gray's Theorem (Hint 1) remains relevant to this day, as I know of two faculty members who had great struggles in promotion and tenure because the demands of the institution were not met by ignoring this singular word of advice. When I showed them *What They Didn't Teach You in Graduate School*, they simply thought it wouldn't have applied to their case but now they know better.

Since you're reading this book, you have probably taken the road into academia. In order to move beyond surviving, into thriving, and into total bliss, this book is your roadmap. Dive in, consult the relevant chapters each semester, and enjoy the humor.

Ryan Nivens
Professor of Mathematics Education
East Tennessee State University

Introduction

Graduate school is a wonderful, heady time for students, particularly those working toward the highest achievement, the PhD. It is a time when long-term friendships are formed, and a time when the discussion in seminars, classes, and with other graduate students focuses on intellectual life. Yes, there are financial worries, given the expenses and the low pay. Yes, there are the problems of maturing for students fresh out of undergraduate school, and the problems of re-entering academia after a long time away from it for students over 30. Nonetheless, it is a marvelous time in your life, and one that you, like today's professors, will look back on fondly.

When you receive the degree and find your first job, you will be exposed to the realities of academic life. What will it be like? How should you navigate this particular real world you are thrust into? Most students, even those who taught part-time before their degree, have only the vaguest concept of that world. It is the purpose of this book to reduce the uncertainty, to present an irreverent guide to what it is *really* like, at least as seen by the authors who each spent a long time immersed in this world as well as in the world outside academia.

360 HINTS: A FULL CIRCLE REVIEW OF LIFE IN ACADEMIA

We deliberately kept this book short, by presenting it in its first edition in the form of 199 hints about what no one told you in graduate school but what you really need to know. In the 16 years since then we have developed an additional 161 hints (bringing the total to 360), mostly reflecting changes in the higher education landscape, for example, the range of changes brought about by advances in digital technology.

Throughout the book, we present data that apply to the median of the book's anticipated readership. Because we fully realize the median is representative rather than universal, we qualify many statements with words such as usually, because you, the reader, may differ extensively from the median.

Some of the hints are short, others longer. Some of the individual hints are worthy of chapters or books of their own, whereas others are important tidbits to tuck into your head for future reference. We've tried to write the hints with a bit of humor here and there. Don't be put off by that. What we say is indeed true.

Since we suspect you will keep this book and keep referring to it as you face new situations, we've organized the hints into 16 short chapters and 4 appendices. We've added a numerical list of the hints at the beginning so you can find hints when you need them.

This book is written in terms of our experience in the United States. That is the universe we know. We recognize that procedures, rules, and assumptions differ by country, even those as close as Canada and Mexico. If you are outside the United States and are reading this book, please pardon our parochialism.

Our hints are based on what we see today in the world around us. They do not reflect the way we think academia should be or could be. Unfortunately, or fortunately, depending on your point of view, academia moves slowly. Therefore, much of what is in this book will stand you in good stead for a considerable fraction of your career. Changes are in the wind that may affect you. For example, many argue that tenure will not be here forever. Yet, in the short term you will need to deal with it, and we included a chapter about it.

A particular reality of academia is that in a number of fields, jobs for fresh PhDs are scarce. Although you don't like to think about it in pure business terms, the market for PhDs depends on supply and demand and is notoriously difficult to model and predict. Students make decisions about the field they want to enter years before they complete their degrees. Hence you play a futures game in a changing environment. We do know, however, to use that tired cliche: what goes out of fashion comes back into fashion.

The authors come from research institutions that highly value teaching, as do we. We observe that those with strong research productivity are hired for the most-prized and best-paid positions in higher education. We also observe that many new PhDs see teaching as their highest calling and want to spend their life doing it. Fortunately, the largest employers of faculty are the four-year and community colleges that value teaching first.

In this book we talk not only about the mechanics of being a professor, but also the nature of life as an academic. The next six paragraphs present our view of that life.

At colleges or universities, life is divided arbitrarily into semesters or quarters. For convenience, we talk in terms of semesters. Even at the smallest of schools, at the beginning of each semester you (and your students) face new students whom you've never seen before and many of whom you will never see again in class. Classes meet on a heartbeat schedule—for example, Monday, Wednesday, and Friday for one hour—for a fixed number of weeks. Then it is all over, and you start again. After the spring semester, if you don't teach summer school, you are free to do what you want. For most academics, summer becomes a time to prepare for the next academic year and to do research and, perhaps, take some vacation. But summer is soon over, and you start again.

Whereas students change from semester to semester, your faculty colleagues change only slowly. Yes, some people move on or retire, and new people are brought in to take their place (just as you were), but tomorrow's faculty is like today's faculty, only slightly different. They are people you must live with and who must live with you over considerable periods of time. Then there's the administration and the staff, who, like your colleagues, also change only slowly.

With few exceptions, when you take your first job you are off to a new school, often distant from where you formed strong friendships and learned your profession. Like many PhDs starting out, you may find you are the only one in your department who is deep into your specialty in your field. After all, it was your specialty you were hired for.

You will spend a considerable part of your first year just learning about the school and its norms, establishing a social network of people you trust and are compatible with, and preparing the courses you are assigned to teach. If in a research-intensive school, you will also be expected to advance your research; if in a teaching institution, your teaching load will be heavier, and you will serve on more committees. You will also learn about the quality of the students you teach.

It is a good life, and you even get paid.

Many universities offer preparing future faculty (PFF) programs for PhD students. Although the name may differ from school to school, the objective of these programs is essentially the same as this book: to tell PhD students about the world they will soon enter. If your university offers such a program, enroll. You will learn much that is vital for success as a professor.

We've enjoyed writing these hints and hope you will find them useful. We look forward to receiving feedback from you, favorable and unfavorable, confirming or disagreeing with our advice.

Chapter 1
Basic Concepts

Hint 1 Gray's Theorem $N + 2$. The number of papers required for tenure is $N + 2$, where N is the number you published.

Each year PhD candidates and young faculty members come into our offices and sheepishly ask us to tell them what they really need to know about building a career in academia. We usually take them to a long lunch and give them the helpful hints we share with you in this book.

1. Gray's Theorem $N + 2$. The number of papers required for tenure is $N + 2$, where N is the number you published.

Corollary: Gray's Theorem is independent of N.

2. Most academic fields are dominated by fewer than 100 powerful people. These people know one another and determine the course of the field. Early in your career you should get to know as many of them as possible. More to the point, they should know who you are. You want them to see you as a bright young person at the forefront of your field. Although this tactic is important, be aware of the dangers associated with it. You should not begin the process until after you have mastered the literature (particularly the papers they wrote!) and developed some ideas of your own. If they get to know you and conclude you have no ideas, you're finished.

3. How to become known. Think of whom you know in the field:

- People who write books
- People who publish articles
- People who are active in their professional societies

Use this list as a guide for deciding what you can do to become one of the known people.

4. Drew's Law on publishing papers. Every paper can be published somewhere. Your first papers will be rejected. Don't worry about this. View the reviewer's complete misunderstanding of your brilliance as cheap editorial help. Use their advice to revise. Every paper has a market. If *Journal A* rejects it, make the appropriate changes and send it to *Journal B*. If the work is sound, someone will publish it.

5. Make sure you have at least one mentor early in your career. The old apprentice system still exists. Try to find mentors who were successful with others, who will support you, and who believe that furthering your career helps their own careers. Such a mentor is preferable to the internationally famous Nobel Prize winner who exploits or ignores you.

6. Feldman's Rule of Mentoring. Your mentor should believe more in you than you believe in yourself. Caution: Your mentor might get frustrated. This frustration is not *at* you, but rather at the situation. They are trying to help you anticipate the challenges you will face in your career and prepare you to confront those challenges successfully.

7. Specialize—get known for *something*. It helps visibility. Sadly, brilliant restless people who work on several topics simultaneously usually do not achieve as much visibility as those who plod along in the same area for many years.

8. Trust (yourself and others). You may feel that you were admitted to your graduate program, or hired for your tenure-track position, by mistake—that if they only knew your true capabilities they would not have selected you . . . or that if your work product is not perfect (see Hint 158), you will be "found out." This is called the Imposter Syndrome. Almost always that insecure feeling is wrong; they knew who they were admitting or hiring. But it is shocking to realize how many graduate students and faculty members erroneously feel like imposters.

Grad school and your first job are each a rollercoaster of emotions. It's OK to not be okay. Everyone feels lost at one stage or another and that is okay. You'll have moments of elation and moments of despair, but through perseverance and a mindset of accomplishing your goals it can be done. When it gets tough, that is when you will find out what you are made of. Grad school, especially the dissertation, is largely about perseverance.

Sometimes, you just need to realize that the process works—it has worked for others and it will work for you. This does not mean that you should let the process take advantage of you—you should not. Trust the process *and* your instincts. If it feels like you are being taken advantage of, then you probably are.

9. Always treat people with respect. A life lesson we have learned, and thus put it up front in this first chapter: How you do something usually is more important than what you do. There are people who can hire someone and the new employee leaves their office feeling lousy. And there are others who can fire someone, and that person emerges from the meeting feeling good! As Maya Angelou said, "I've learned that people will forget what you said, people will forget what you did, but people will never forget how you made them feel." This applies to your work in each of the roles we discuss in this book.

10. Above all, try also to have fun. No explanation needed on this hint. Enjoy the journey!

Chapter 2
The PhD

Hint 25 Avoid Watson's Syndrome, a euphemism for procrastination.

It can be argued that you do job hunting (the subject of Chapter 4) before you receive the PhD. However, the PhD is the prize you seek above all from your graduate experience. We therefore discuss it first.

11. Job preparation. Your assigned advisor may not be the best fit for you. As you progress in your program, build relationships with other professors, ask curious questions; don't be afraid to be that person who wants to study an area that no one else focuses on.

12. Cobble together your own mentors inside and outside your department. Mentors serve different purposes and can provide guidance at different times in your career. While you knew you were capable of getting your graduate degree, you may not be sure what you want to do with it. Especially if you are getting a PhD—academia is not the only path. There are many practical applications of a PhD that might open a different world of opportunities for you.

13. Keep your class notes and books. Resist the urge to rent books. Regardless of your job, once you have it, much of what you learned in class will have elevated relevance—keep all of your lecture notes and textbooks.

14. Finish your PhD as early as possible while gaining the most experience that you can within the safety net of graduate school. Don't feel you need to create the greatest work that Western civilization ever saw. Five years from now the only thing that will matter is that you finished. If you don't finish, you are likely to join the ranks of freeway flyers, holding multiple part-time teaching jobs.

15. You are never too old and it is never too late. While time might seem in conflict with Hint 14, the idea here is to "Just Do It" (famous Nike phrase). You may even find that you have more focus and drive when you are older. One of the authors got their PhD later in life (it was a 50th birthday present to themself) and they have never looked back . . . and never regretted not getting it earlier.

16. Be humble about your PhD. You don't need to flaunt the degree. Everyone has one. Many of your colleagues in your institution and outside it will be put off if you sign everything Dr. or Jane Jones, PhD. In fact, the main use for the title of doctor is making reservations at a restaurant. When you call and ask for a table for four for Dr. Jones, you will get more respect and often better seating.

17. Maybe you *are* a teacher. There are times when using PhD in your title may be off-putting. Think about certain social situations where the majority of people there have not gone to college, for example, the parents in your child's playgroup. Sometimes, it is easier to say that you are a teacher (which is really what you are). This will likely lead to a follow on questions about where you teach and then you can say XYZ University.

18. A PhD is primarily an indication of survivorship and perseverance. Although the public at large may view your doctorate as a superb intellectual achievement and a reflection of brilliance, you probably know deep in your heart that it is not. It represents a lot of hard work on your part over a long period of time. You probably received help from one or more faculty members to get over rough spots. Your family, be it parents or spouse, stayed with you over the vicissitudes of creating the dissertation. You stuck with it until it was done, unlike the ABDs (all but dissertations) people who complete all the other requirements, but bail out before they finish their dissertations.

19. Avoid using the term "ABD" to refer to yourself. It means "All But Dissertation." The original meaning of ABD referred to people who completed all the other requirements, but never finished the dissertation. It is a pejorative term and usually indicates a longer-term status than the time between your proposal and your graduation. These days some students describe themselves that way to signal that they only have the dissertation left to do before they receive their PhD. But most people who hear them will attach the old, disparaging, meaning to that term. The correct term, which shows progress towards completion of your degree, is "Advanced to Candidacy" or "PhD Candidate."

20. A PhD is a certification of independent research ability based on a sample of one. The PhD certifies that you are able to do quality research. Unlike the MD, which requires extensive work with patients followed by years of internship and residency, the PhD is based on a single sample: your dissertation. The people who sign your dissertation are making a large bet on your ability to do quality independent research again and again in the future.

21. A PhD is a license to reproduce. It is also an obligation to maintain the quality of your intellectual descendants. Once you are a PhD, it is possible for you (assuming you are working in an academic department that offers a PhD program) to create new PhDs. Even if your department does not offer a PhD, you can be called upon to sit on PhD examining committees in your own or in neighboring institutions. Yours is a serious responsibility because you are creating your intellectual descendants. Remember that if you vote to pass someone who is marginal or worse, that PhD in turn is given the same privilege. If candidates are not up to standard, it is likely that some of their descendants will not be also. Unlike humans whose intergeneration time is 20 years, academic intergeneration time is 5 years or less. Furthermore, a single individual may supervise 50 or more PhDs over a 30-year career.

22. You must have the PhD in hand before you can move up the academic ladder. The world is full of ABDs. We talked about them briefly in Hints 18 and 19 and will again in Hint 34. ABDs may be more able and more brilliant than you are, but they didn't possess the stamina (or the circumstances) to finish the degree. In our judgment, being an ABD is the end of the academic line.

23. Anticipate the key danger point in your PhD studies. The key danger point is where you leave highly structured course work (Phase 1) and enter the unstructured world of the qualification examination and the dissertation (Phase 2). Here are strategies to help you navigate Phase 2.

- Stay in touch. Communicate with your professors, especially your adviser. One of us insists that students come in for a meeting each week, even if nothing happened. Just the fear of not being able to report anything stimulates the mind.
- Find a person or two in your cohort with whom you can commiserate. Having support from family or friends is also important, but that person within your cohort understands at a level that others won't. Once you find your person, invite them to be your editing and dissertation buddy. The benefit of a dissertation buddy cannot be overstated.
- Meet regularly, ideally every week, for lunch or dinner or afternoon coffee, with two or three fellow graduate students who are also struggling with Phase 2. Compare notes and progress.

24. The PhD and part-time study. Although all PhD students used to be on a campus and often worked as teaching or research assistants part-time, in many fields that attract midcareer or executive students today (for example, education) the norm is to work at an off-campus job full-time and on the PhD part-time. Others, such as computer science students, develop an idea for a start-up company (e.g., the cofounders of Google) and drift from full-time to part-time. We applaud part-time PhD students!

If you are working on your PhD part-time, you will find it difficult enough in Phase 1 to tell your boss that you can't attend that nighttime budget crisis meeting or tell your spouse that you can't go to your child's soccer game because you must be in class. It is even more difficult when you're in Phase 2 to tell them that you won't be there because you must be home, in your study, staring at a blank computer screen trying to get past writer's block.

As a part-time student, you need to find ways to be physically present on campus. You can do so in many ways, such as spending time writing in a library carrel.[1] Physical presence is important psychologically. If you never visit campus and become caught up in your work and family activities, you face the danger that your uncompleted PhD program can begin to seem like something you used to do in a faraway time and place.

25. Avoid Watson's Syndrome. While originally named by R. J. Gelles for Mr. Watson who remained ABD, this syndrome is a euphemism for procrastination and its relationship to academic performance is well documented in the literature.[2] It involves doing everything possible to avoid completing work. It differs from writer's block in that the sufferer substitutes real work that distracts them from doing what is necessary to complete the dissertation or for advancing toward an academic career. The work may be outside or inside the university. Examples of procrastination originally listed by Gelles include:

- Remodeling a house
- A never-ending literature review (after all, new papers are being published all the time and they must be referenced)
- Data paralysis—making seemingly infinite statistical models

If you suffer from Watson's Syndrome, finding a mentor who pushes you to finish will help you get it done. The importance of this cannot be overstated and thus appears also in Hints 5, 6, 12, 89, and 98). For many, however, particularly those who always waited until the night before an examination to begin studying, the syndrome is professionally fatal.

26. Celebrate your PhD. When you hand in your signed dissertation and pay the last fee the university exacts from you, go out and Celebrate! Celebrate! Celebrate! According to the 2021 US Census Bureau, only about 2 percent of the population 25 years and over have a PhD. You've achieved something marvelous, and you are one of a very small number in the population who can say you are a PhD. Attaining a PhD is a big deal. Honor that.

Celebrations are also called for when you pass your qualifying examination, when your dissertation proposal is accepted, and when you successfully defend your dissertation. Be sure to attend your graduation ceremony so you can share your achievement with your family.

A PhD, like life, is a journey. It marks the end of one stage and the beginning of what lies ahead. Don't fail to appreciate the moment of your accomplishment. Yes, other big moments await you. But like almost every PhD, you never had a moment this big, and it will be a long time before you have another one that matches it.

NOTES

1 The library is a large building filled with books and journals. It functions sort of like Google, but on a deeper level.

2 L. D. Blum (2010) "The 'all-but-the-dissertation' student and the psychology of the doctoral dissertation." *Journal of College Student Psychotherapy*, 24(2): 74–85.

Chapter 3

The Dissertation

Hint 30 Find out about the format well before you take prelims.

We put our thoughts on the dissertation into this early chapter because for readers who are graduate students, the dissertation, including the proposal, is the largest single hurdle they must leap over to achieve the PhD. This chapter is supplemented by Appendix A, which describes the mechanics involved in the end stages of the dissertation process once it has been written and approved by the adviser. The appendix covers the time from the oral defense to handing the dissertation in to the registrar.

If you already have your PhD, you can skip this chapter and Appendix A for now, but they will be of help to you later when you are a member of a PhD advisory committee or when you are mentoring students.

27. Selecting the dissertation advisory committee. Be skillful and strategic in selecting your dissertation advisory committee. The worst possible approach is to pick people because they are famous in their field. Rather, be aware that the role of the advisory committee actually is to help you. Therefore, choose people who can really help you over the rough spots. If your dissertation is experimental and requires expertise in two fields, pick an expert in each field and someone who knows about experimental design and statistics. When push comes to shove (and it will at some time while you are working on your dissertation), the people you need will be there to help you because they made a commitment to you. Simply hoping the expert will contribute time to your problem without being on the committee can prove to be naive.

28. Let your chair help you identify other committee members. You want people who work well together and who, ideally, have been on dissertation committees together in the past. You can look some of these up in the Dissertations and Theses Database, by your school or by members, to see who has worked together. Have an honest conversation with your chair—if you know that stern people increase your anxiety such that you cannot think clearly, having a stern statistician on your committee is likely not a good idea. Your chair will help you sort this out—they know—trust them.

29. Prelims/Qualifying exam. To obtain a PhD almost everyone takes a preliminary, or qualifying, examination, commonly known as prelims or quals. The purpose of prelims is to demonstrate you understand, and can explain, your major field and are sufficiently knowledgeable to undertake a dissertation. You must pass prelims before you can advance to the candidacy level. The number of times you can take prelims is usually limited, although you can petition for another chance. If you fail all attempts, you must leave the graduate program.

The content and format varies by field and by school. In the formal sit-down format you are examined in specified subfields. The exams cover several days, and each part is allocated a fixed time.

30. Format of the prelims. Find out about the format well before you take prelims. Prelims are highly stressful before you take them but most (at least those who pass) remember them afterward as being "trivial" or an "integrating exercise," among other similar descriptions. The stress is real, and few PhD students prepare alone. Students form study groups that meet periodically to compare notes, test one another, prepare sample responses to previous questions, and offer encouragement. Asking students who passed the prelims about their experiences helps reduce anxiety for those about to take them. Knowing who is preparing each question also reduces uncertainty.

In most cases, when you pass all but one part of the prelims, you can petition to retake that part.

31. Determine the best time for you to take prelims. Unless your department or school specifies the timing of your prelims, you have some freedom of choice. If you take them too early (e.g., the semester you arrive) you are likely to fail. If you take them too late or at the last possible moment, you risk increasing the time to degree. If you wait too long, most of the people who arrived the same time as you have already taken them, and your study group will be mostly people you don't know well. Furthermore, since faculty and courses change, prelims' test material is different from year to year. Also, the longer you wait the greater the risk that you have fallen out of the groove of knowledge that is needed to pass these exams.

32. 3-paper versus traditional dissertation. Some schools will allow the student to choose between a 3-paper dissertation or a traditional dissertation. The 3-paper dissertation is one in which the student has three papers at various stages of publication or readiness for publication. This format allows for early publication opportunities and the flexibility and adaptability to do three interrelated projects. This is still presented as a dissertation in one document where the literature review and the discussion of the dissertation address all three papers. There are drawbacks to the 3-paper model that should be understood before deciding on which is best for you. Some disadvantages include integration challenges, publication pressures (you are at the mercy of the reviewers), and variable standards across academia.

A traditional dissertation is one cohesive document that allows for comprehensive exploration of the project. While there is flexibility in presentation of a traditional dissertation, the academic standards are widely accepted. There are drawbacks to a traditional dissertation also, such as pressure for perfection and less immediate feedback from committee members. Traditional dissertations can be perceived as more time-consuming, but we do not believe that to be the case.

33. Primary versus secondary data—what you should know. If you create your own questionnaire for your dissertation research, this is defined as "primary data."

The major advantage of primary data is that you can thoughtfully decide the mapping of the questions to the theoretical constructs and how each item is phrased. And sometimes distributing a survey can go quickly. If you are studying high school mathematics teachers (or guidance counselors, or football coaches), you may find that you can obtain permission to distribute your survey at a regional meeting of math teachers. Ask for 15 minutes of dedicated time at the conference. Don't simply distribute a link or QR code that they can access later. If you can pull this off, you may gather most or all of your data in one fell swoop. The major disadvantage of primary data is that it is difficult, if not impossible, to gather data from a national sample. There are channels, such as posting your survey on multiple social media outlets, which can be used as a mechanism to try to obtain a representative sample. However, there is always a risk (aka limitation) that you will not collect as many responses as you had anticipated.

Secondary data are data that someone else, usually a state or Federal organization, gathered which you can analyze for your study. The two main advantages of using secondary data in your dissertation research are: 1) you can obtain a statewide or national sample, and 2) you can totally skip the data collection phase of your research.

But the primary versus secondary decision involves trade-offs. The big disadvantage of secondary analysis is that you must work with items that someone else developed and likely collected to answer a different question from the one you are trying to answer. Some of the key questions to address your theoretical constructs may not have been included in the survey, and if they were, you may not be happy with the wording. You cannot change that and are stuck with what you have. Also, some, actually few, secondary data files are clean, well-structured and easy for a researcher to use. Others are a mess and can soak up months of your time cleaning, merging (if you have two different data sets), and structuring before you can carry out your first analysis.

34. Finding a dissertation topic is not as easy as it looks. In fact, for a lot of students it is the most difficult part of their dissertation. (Many students begin erroneously believing that defining a topic is supposed to be the easiest part of the dissertation. "If I'm having so much trouble with the easiest part of this task, how will I ever finish?") Some students go to a professor they want to work with and ask for suggestions for a topic. Usually, they wind up desperately unhappy because the topic is not theirs, yet they are condemned to work on it. Often these students spend the rest of their life as ABDs. Over the next many, many months, you will develop an intimate love/hate relationship with the topic—make sure it motivates you or this love/hate relationship becomes all hate.

35. Problem-solving mode. Don't assume that if you are having trouble defining a dissertation topic the entire dissertation process will be that arduous. Once you define the topic, you are in problem-solving mode, and most people do well in solving a problem once they know what the topic is.

36. Review a published dissertation. As you are developing your proposal, take the time to read at least one completed dissertation "from cover to cover." Ideally this would be a dissertation from your own institution and department that is about a subject matter close to your topic. This will help to give you realistic expectations about local standards. Do not be intimidated if you inadvertently select a dissertation that is 300 pages long. Put it back and find a normal dissertation (see Hint 44).

37. Put a lot of effort into writing your dissertation proposal. The proposal is frequently significantly more difficult than the dissertation. The proposal has two important payoffs, so take your time and be thorough.

- It usually provides one or more chapters of your end product, the dissertation.
- It is a contract between you and your advisory committee on what you must do to receive the degree. In general, if you do what you promise in the proposal well, the committee should sign the final document.

If you cannot accomplish all you set out to do, it is up to you to communicate with your chair first, then your committee. If you have to make a methodological change because of unforeseen circumstances beyond your control, the proposal has specified the goals and the research questions. These can assist in evaluating, for example, a new sample or a modified approach. Many students during the COVID-19 pandemic, for example, lost all access to people. So, if their dissertations involved people, with the help of their dissertation chair, they learned the fine art of pivoting, reframing, or condensing . . . or they are still working on their dissertations.

38. There are always limitations. Although the limitations encountered by students during COVID-19 could have never been predicted, many limitations can be predicted. You are expected to include a "Limitations" section in both your proposal and your dissertation. In your proposal, the limitations may be something like "A request for data has been submitted to the state of Massachusetts; however, it has yet to be approved." In the full dissertation, the limitations usually are presented in Chapter 5 of the dissertation. Be honest in this section. For example, "While this was a study about the ways in which external political factors affect the teaching of American history in high school, the sample of history teachers was drawn entirely from Florida. These issues may have a different impact on teachers from Massachusetts or California." However, don't stray into self-abasement in this section. State the limitations clearly and succinctly, and then move on.

39. Your positionality statement. Many students now include a positionality statement in both their proposal and the dissertation itself. Some departments require it. This section describes why you became interested in this subject and the experiences and beliefs that you bring to it. This is both a chance to express the roots of your passion for the topic and one way to guard against injecting bias into your research.

40. The proposed timeline. Whether required or not, it is always a good idea to present a proposed timeline of your research during the proposal defense. Try to be realistic. The department wants you to do thoughtful planning and be successful. All too frequently, students present a timeline that is hopelessly optimistic. If you do this, you probably are creating unrealistic expectations for yourself. This can lead to disappointment and to you perceiving your dissertation research as more difficult than it is, when, in reality, given a realistic timeline, it really was not that difficult.

41. The range of your literature review. If little or nothing is written on your dissertation topic, don't assume that an abbreviated literature review is acceptable. Dissertation committees are used to a minimum-size review and will insist on it. If only three previous papers even touch on your subject, reviewing just them is not considered an adequate literature search. Furthermore, the new data you expect to obtain, even in a specialized topic, can affect a lot of intersecting, and even some parallel, fields. Those fields should be identified. In short, a literature review not only discusses what is already done and why, it also points out the areas where your work has implications.

42. The dissertation abstract. Once you have completed a good presentable dissertation draft, it is time to write your abstract.

Do not underestimate the importance of the abstract—it is more than a bureaucratic afterthought. Many people who you think might be reading your entire dissertation will only be reading the abstract—make it count! They include people who might hire you, such as faculty on search committees and deans at institutions where you may apply for jobs.

Your institution limits abstracts to a maximum number of words. Unfortunately, a short abstract is more difficult to write than a long one. Try to summarize your research question, methods, and key findings succinctly and accurately. Also, think of the abstract as a public relations statement. Include references to powerful theories you tested, impressive models you applied or developed, and advanced techniques you employed. Don't be shy.

43. Your concluding paragraphs. Your dissertation should conclude with a strong paragraph, or paragraphs. State your major conclusions and stress how the world would be improved if your recommendations were implemented. Whatever you do, do not end your dissertation with the Limitations section.

44. How long is too long for your dissertation? How short is too short? No strict guidelines exist for the length of a dissertation. Because field and institutional differences exist, we can only provide generic guidelines.

In our experience, the median length for the body of a dissertation is about 125 double-spaced pages. (This figure does not include the abstract, front matter, references or appendices.) We estimate that 80 percent of the dissertations we have seen ran between 90 and 150 pages of main text. The length tends to be at the short end in the sciences and at the long end in the humanities.

We strongly believe dissertation quality is always more important than dissertation length. We are sure your faculty committee members agree.

45. The chain of references is vital in doing a literature search. Begin with one or two recent articles, (a survey article helps), and look at the references that are cited. Then read the publications that seem apropos and look at their reference lists. Repeat this process. Some things will pop up often, and they are usually (but not invariably) the classics in the field that you must include in your references. Proceed from reference to reference until the law of diminishing returns takes over.

46. Match the literature search to the discussion of results and the conclusions. You may find that as your dissertation progresses, some parts of your literature search are really irrelevant to your research. In this case, you should be ruthless. Despite the brilliance of your prose and the long, tedious hours you put into creating the material, you must delete these pearls. Of course, you should save what you don't use as part of your file of references (Hint 156) so you can use it over and over in future publications.

47. The risk of results that are not significant. When you select a dissertation topic and write a proposal, be it qualitative or quantitative, you confidently expect to obtain statistically significant results. Significance involves two dimensions:

- The results are statistically significant.
- The results are important to the field or produce new insights and understandings.

It is perfectly possible that your results don't show the effect you predicted, or the analysis does not meet standard statistical significance tests. This risk, although usually small, is there in all dissertations; it's a form of the promise-performance gap.

What do you do if it happens to you? In almost every case, you shouldn't give up or quit your pursuit of the PhD. Follow Plan B. Yes, you must convince your adviser (and your committee) that you needn't start over. But you obtained a lot of data during your work, and the data can be used to show, for example, that:

- The methodology you used is correct, but the desired effect is not there with this methodology in your particular sample
- With a meta-analysis based on adding your results to others, the existing theory is stronger (or weaker) than previously thought
- An analysis that is not statistically significant for the entire sample is significant for an important subgroup
- Your results, while not statistically significant, might be practically or operationally significant

Moreover, approval of your dissertation should not require that you find statistical significance. If a scientist carries out rigorous analyses, they might obtain nonsignificant results, although it is important to note that larger samples (i.e. power) might result in statistical significance. This does not mean that the results do not have some practical significance. This is especially true in applied dissertations. Moreover, if the data suggest or imply or illustrate anything at all, you should turn to the word, "heuristic." According to the Merriam-Webster Dictionary, this word means "involving or serving as an aid to learning, discovery, or problem-solving . . ." "Although the analyses yielded no correlations that were statistically significant, the results are still of great heuristic value and may advance thinking about this subject." Own it and write about it with confidence.

48. The dissertation defense. The dissertation oral defense before an august group of senior faculty is almost always a love feast. Most advisers won't let their students into the examination room if there is even a one-in-a-million chance they will fail. Remember, the adviser's reputation is on the line as well as yours.

When you're finished with your dissertation, you know more about the subject than anyone else in the room. If you suspect that someone on the committee hadn't yet read your dissertation, be kind and explain it in "See Dick. See Jane. See Dick and Jane run up the hill" terms.

If you can't answer a question, say so. Don't fumble and stumble. The inquisitor will ask another one. One of us recalls their own oral defense, which at that time consisted of a defense of the dissertation and any questions examiners chose to ask. A true *éminence grise* in the field asked about a topic he was the world's expert on, and the student knew little about it. After taking it as far as possible, the student said, "That's all I know." The expert then inquired if the student's significant other was in the sciences. When the student said no, he asked, "How do you explain your field to your significant other?" The student admired the question as he answered it. The expert voted pass.

Unfortunately, there is always that one faculty member in the audience who feels the need to show that *they, not you* are the expert on this topic. Let them talk and then graciously say something like, "You bring up some interesting points that I will look into." Do not go to battle with them—you will lose.

Chapter 4
Job Hunting

Hint 81 When interviewing, try to find out whether the members of the faculty like one another.

The hints in this chapter are directed primarily at those who seek to earn their living in academe. To get in, you must first be offered a job, and that first job will strongly affect the rest of your academic life. If you decide you don't want to go into academe or you don't find a job, see Hint 72. If you become unemployed, see Hint 94.

49. Job hunting is a research project. You should treat it as such. Gather as much information as possible. Read the ads. Contact sources. Follow up leads. Be aggressive. Use your contacts and your social and digital presence (see Hints 2 and 256). The chance of landing a good appointment is greater if you search broadly than if you sit in your office waiting for one or two possibilities. Begin job hunting early and make it a project you do along with your other work. If you are a graduate student, don't wait until your dissertation is finished to start looking (but see Hint 52).

50. Pick a place where you and your family want to live that matches your lifestyle. City people are not happy in isolated college towns, and small-town people find it hard to adjust to a megalopolis. For more on this, see Hints 88 and 103.

51. When to apply for a faculty position. For PhD candidates, the timing of your job application will be determined by your progress in completing the degree and your financial situation.

All things being equal, we recommend applying while you are nearing completion of your degree, after your proposal is approved, and you are well along on your dissertation. But don't wait until your dissertation is completed, approved, and turned in. Although you don't want job hunting to interfere with the successful completion of your dissertation, you don't want to graduate and then wonder where you will work next year.

52. Find the best possible school for your first job. You can only go down in the pecking order, not up, if you don't make it at your first position. If you are a success, you can go up one level at a time. Officials at Stanford University don't typically hire from Succotash Community College, for example.

53. Change your field or move every seven years if you really want a broader challenge. This advice seems to run counter to our advice to obtain tenure as soon as possible. It is not. As we say in Hints 184 and 185, tenure can be negotiated on the way in.

So why change? It improves salary possibilities. At higher education institutions, people are hired at the national market rate and are given raises, based on the internal annual percentage increase, which are usually negligible. Moving is often the only way to maintain parity or gain a major increase in salary and perquisites.

Change also broadens your outlook. Some broadening is the result of the Hawthorne Effect. That is, people pay attention to you because you are new. In the first few years at the new institution or department you will have the aura of the outside expert. After a while, you are just one of the same old crowd.

Changing fields allows you to move from a mature area to a new dynamic one. That's where the fun is. It is also an opportunity to get in on the ground floor of a new development. However, you must be careful. Move only to adjacent fields where you can use most of your tools and leverage existing knowledge, because changing careers involves some retooling. Radical swings such as moving from French to cognitive psychology or electrical engineering are usually impossible without a second PhD.

54. Not-for-profit or for-profit for your first or second job?[1] Most US colleges and universities, whether public or private, are nonprofit, which means they can make a profit but they can't give it to anyone. In particular, they can't give it to stockholders because there aren't any. They rely on government funding—usually research funding—endowments, and private donations to make up the difference between tuition income and expenses.

Stockholders or owners of for-profit colleges seek to maximize their return from their investments. A 2010 US Government sampling of for-profits found extensive fraud, particularly in obtaining government support for students.[2]

There are a lot of for-profit educational institutions. An incomplete list in Wikipedia in 2024 showed 109 for-profits with another 66 having closed since the 2010 report.[3] Many of the for-profits have multiple locations offering everything from associate degrees to PhDs, from liberal arts to medicine. The two largest for-profit universities are the University of Phoenix and Grand Canyon University, both with multiple locations and both with their main location in Phoenix, AZ.

If you've spent years obtaining your PhD and worked in a research environment, you will find that most for-profit jobs focus primarily on teaching, with standardized course content you have no say about.

Should you become involved with them? Our first response is no (but see our next hint). They'll pay much less than the nonprofits and the environment will be different than that of a nonprofit college or university. For example, with the focus on teaching, you will have less research time, if any at all. In our opinion, the downside far exceeds the benefits.

55. Exceptions to the previous hint. If you're a graduate student who needs teaching experience or needs to supplement your munificent doctoral stipend, for-profit schools give you instant experience. Often your students are mature, older than you, and far more interested in your subject than 18–22-year-old undergraduates.

If you have your PhD in hand but not the academic job you long for, a for-profit can be a stopgap. It will supplement your unemployment insurance (if you're eligible) while giving you additional teaching experience. However, we have two caveats if you later want a permanent appointment in a nonprofit:

- To be hired later by a school with a strong research requirement for its tenure track, keep your research going—this is essential
- For an appointment in a teaching institution, become an adjunct in a nonprofit college to show you have teaching experience in that sector

In either case, tell the nonprofit's search committee you took the for-profit job to improve your teaching skills while looking for the right place to spend your career. Remember, nonprofit faculty almost invariably look down their noses at the for-profits, in part because they compete with them.

56. Prepare your CV carefully. CVs and résumés are important, but know the difference. For an academic job, you must submit a CV, a "Curriculum Vitae" and not a résumé. In any case, they are your entrée to the process. Invest in having yours done professionally. It should be neat, but not gaudy. Include everything that is remotely relevant. Some search committees use a checklist of skills, experiences, and other criteria they expect for a position. Do you know something about, say, medieval literature or databases, which the department might want you to teach? A committee may blindly drop you from consideration if its members don't put a checkmark next to each of their items. Your problem is that the list of items is different at every institution. Also, many universities have CV templates that you can find online. Consider putting your CV on their template to make it easier for the search committee to follow your accomplishments (give them something that is familiar).

A key part of your CV (or an attachment to it) will be your reference list. Some search committee members prefer to talk with references rather than to read your publications.

To get a job (and tenure later) you will need references beyond those of your dissertation committee. Build a reference pool; that is, identify people who will say nice things about you. They needn't be famous or distinguished, but they should hold impressive titles or be employed at prestigious places. References from abroad are particularly desirable since they show you to be a person with some international reputation in your field. Remember that administrators of universities are lazy. When references are needed, they will ask you for a long list of names to choose from. Pick your friends.

57. Dual careers. If you have a spouse or significant other with a career, you may have obstacles to accepting a good offer. Dual careers usually mean that two jobs are needed. This situation is particularly difficult if the spouse is also an academic, and you require two appointments, say, in biochemistry and political science. In rare and usually only senior cases, the university quickly approves a spousal hire. Most departments making an offer to one spouse will try to assist the second (or "trailing") spouse in locating an academic appointment. But that is a tough game to play. Ironically, universities often conclude years later that the trailing spouse has made more contributions to the institution than the spouse they originally hired.

58. The short list. Search committees receive many more applications than they can deal with, and they prefer to deal with just a few. Therefore, their usual procedure is to create a short list of candidates to consider further. To be on the short list, you need to stand out from the crowd.

The procedure varies from search to search. Sometimes the committee checks references before inviting a short-listed candidate to campus, sometimes after.[4] Sometimes committee members conduct interviews by video conference before choosing whom to invite to campus. So, in your application:

- Don't be modest. Make sure your major achievements are highlighted in your CV and your cover letter.
- It's shocking, but some search committee members read only the cover letters. Craft each cover letter carefully. Specify how your work relates to the requirements of the specific job and what you feel your contributions might be to the department.
- Follow all instructions. Some committees winnow applicants by removing any application that omits anything they asked for, such as a statement about your philosophy of teaching.
- Ask for your reference letters early. The main reason some applications are set aside is that the folder is incomplete because a reference you suggested is missing, even though that reference would have been top notch. That is, the position requires three reference letters, but the institution has only received two.

Once your application package is complete, proofread it (Hint 151). Tiny errors, like misspellings or a wrong date can keep you off the short list.[5] A note of caution: If you are applying to multiple schools and using the same cover letter, double and triple check that the proper name is on the cover letter.

59. The campus visit. Once you've applied for a position and made it to the short list, you may be selected as a finalist and asked to come to campus for an interview and job talk (presentation). In addition to reading this set of hints, also read the ones about data gathering, because some of that data is best gathered during your interview.

60. Tactics for interviewing. You may start out self-confidently on your first interview assuming you can wing it, or you are so timid that you just know you're going to fail. In either case, you will run into portions of the interview that go like a charm and other parts that don't. Fortunately, almost everybody gets more than one interview. Just like teaching (Hint 97), being interviewed is a learned art.

Remember, you are only going to accept one job, but you will (hopefully) be interviewed by many. You will have to deal with rejection, but you most likely learned how to do that when you applied to multiple graduate schools.

The secret to landing a job is to try for many and not be intimidated or crushed by rejections, which are inevitable. This means you will likely lose out on many job competitions before you finally land a good position . . . and the right position.

The most important part of interviewing as a finalist for an academic position is the job talk, which is usually a lecture about your research. Prepare your presentation carefully. *Rehearse it, preferably in front of friends.* Ask for their comments and criticisms.

61. Dressing for the job interview. With a tough job market, a lot depends on the initial interview. The initial, and later, interview outcomes often depend on the impression you make when you walk into the room. Don't turn the interviewers off before you even start talking. All the person knows about you is in the CV you sent and how you look. The adage clothes make the person is still true.

Admittedly if you are a graduate student who has lived hand to mouth for years, dressed in a wardrobe of jeans and Birkenstocks, you may not have the right clothes in your closet. If you don't, go to a local clothes outlet or even a thrift shop and use a credit card if necessary. Make sure the clothes fit. This investment pays off.

62. Wardrobe color. Find something in your wardrobe that represents the school's colors. It could be a tie or a scarf or even a pattern in the fabric. It should be subtle, but it shows that you know the school and you are one with the culture.

63. Don't be intimidated by the schools your interviewers attended. Before interviewing at a particular institution, look in the catalog to find out where faculty received their doctorates. Don't be fooled by the names of the schools. Even top schools graduate mediocre people who do nothing once they obtain a PhD. On the other hand, others are world-class scholars who would be delightful colleagues but may have attended no-name institutions.

64. Be discriminating. You want to work with pleasant people who have good ideas, a good work ethic, and who value honesty and cooperation.

Here are some warning signs to help you make decisions about the people you meet at the interview. Be wary of those who do the following:

- Use a three-syllable word when one syllable will do
- Make too big a deal out of where the person received their PhD

- Cause you to sense that you can't trust the person
- Make disparaging remarks about their colleagues
- Ask intrusive personal questions, such as about your relationship status or your age (both are illegal)

65. Who is interviewing whom? Remember that they are interviewing you and you are interviewing them. Come prepared by having researched every person in the department and every person with whom you will interview. Make sure you have your list of questions, but recognize that researchers love to talk about themselves. If you listen closely enough, you will find out all you need to know about them. It is critical that you see your potential at this location and with these people . . . they will be your colleagues. Does this place feel like a place where you can grow and flourish? Are there enough resources? For example, if they are going to require you do bring in 30 percent of your salary in funded research or grants, what is the grants support that is provided? If there is no support, then you are doing everything yourself and this process can have a very steep learning curve and can take an enormous amount of time.

66. Dealing with interviewers who have published less than you have. If you are a new PhD or an active researcher, it is possible that those who are interviewing you may have published less than you or in less prestigious journals. Don't be judgmental as you do not know the circumstances of their appointment. Stress the importance of your research but don't overwhelm them with the details unless they start asking questions.

67. Prepare an elevator speech. Imagine you are attending a national conference. You step into an express elevator on the 45th floor of the building and push the lobby button. The only other person in the elevator is, say, the senior federal policy maker in your area of interest, someone from the National Endowment for the Humanities, the US president's science adviser, or the chair of the department where you really want a job. The person says that they heard you completed an important dissertation study and would like to know about your research, but because of a packed schedule, the person only has the time of this elevator ride to learn about your work. What do you tell that person? For one of the authors, this was one of the best pieces of advice by her dissertation chair and it has paid off over and over again.

JOBS

This section focuses on the types of employment available for new and recent PhDs beyond the usual academic appointments in a college or university. These options should help you to decide which kinds of job to look for. The problem is one of information: obtaining information about available jobs for you and potential employers' obtaining information about you. The next hints focus on your information needs.

68. You want information about your availability to reach employers you haven't yet considered. An important way of doing so is making your CV broadly accessible. LinkedIn is a terrific place for announcing that you are looking for work and making your CV available (see Hint 256). For academic jobs, some professional societies compile collections of CVs of members (including student members) looking for employment and make them available to schools that are hiring in their members' specialties. Find out if this is true in your field. If you are seeking a new position, make sure you are on your professional society's list. Also, find out which professional meetings (Hint 93) include recruiting.

69. The law of supply and demand applies to academia as much as to other fields. You are playing a futures game on the job market, no different from a high roller in the stock market, when you select a field of study for your PhD. Since it takes several years to acquire the degree, you make the assumption that your services will be in demand several years from now. Fields move in and out of favor over time. When a hot new field or specialty opens up, it is an exciting time. Lots of people wander in from adjacent fields. They form departments or concentration areas and begin training PhDs in that specialty. People are in short supply, and salaries are good. However, what usually happens is that within a relatively short period of time, the PhD market becomes saturated, and jobs become scarcer. Furthermore, other new specialties emerge, and schools cut back on the previous fad. Examples that have been evolving and redefining themselves are Data Science and Artificial Intelligence (AI). Both are popular fields made possible by the increased power, speed, and massive memory options of supercomputers that are capable of handling the volume and velocity of data. There is a debate about the degree to which these fields are simply a rebranding of Statistics and Computer Science, respectively. Higher education has responded with a variety of majors, concentrations, degree programs, and institutes bearing one or both of these names. Time will tell whether academic jobs for data scientists and AI continue to proliferate, or, alternatively, whether the field will reach saturation. One of the authors has written about how these issues play out in Data Science (available at: https://scholarship.claremont.edu/jhm/vol14/iss1/20).

70. The assistant dean strategy. If your field suffers from an oversupply of people, one strategy is to seek a job as an assistant dean. This approach is quite tricky. Colleges are always looking for candidates for such necessary but non-glorious jobs as assistant dean for student affairs or assistant dean of administration or assistant dean for summer school. As an applicant, you should insist that you also receive an appointment (even if not tenure track) in your field of specialty, say, history. You should also insist that you teach one course or that you are given some time for research. Unless you do so, you will never be given a crack at a tenure-track position. You must then be active in your department and be seen by the department as a member in good standing who gives it access to the administration. Even then, you may never be fully accepted (see Hint 221). However, you will gain experience that can be used later, and you will gain the academic title (and the teaching and research experience) needed on your CV when you look for a job involving full-time teaching and research.

71. Evaluate a postdoc carefully, particularly if you are in the sciences. You should think of a postdoc in cold, hard economic terms. It is an investment (or speculation, depending on your point of view) just like buying stocks or real estate. You will certainly be paid less than if you took a teaching position, but you may gain additional knowledge and experience to make more money in the long run in your chosen field. The anticipated benefits must exceed the short-run costs to make the investment worthwhile, especially if the post-doc is at a school that is equivalent to or a step down from that which you graduated. A postdoc is appropriate under the following conditions:

- You are in a field where jobs at good places are scarce and you did not get one, or you delayed too long in starting your job search
- You feel you need to gain specific research tools (or, if you're a scientist, experience with specialized equipment) to be able to move your research past your PhD dissertation
- You want to work with a specific individual (preferably one of the powerful 100; see Hint 2) who will further your growth
- You want to build up your publication list without using up your tenure clock (see Hint 192)

A postdoc is not appropriate if you are afraid of teaching or talking in front of people. You are merely delaying the inevitable—confronting your fears or anxieties about presenting. See Hint 101 for help. A postdoc is also not appropriate if you are tired of living on a shoestring for years while working on your PhD or are trying to support a family. You may need to find a higher paying nonacademic job.

72. Non-academic opportunities. You may find as you go through your job search that you don't really want to work in academe, or you may be one of the unlucky ones who doesn't find the right assistant professorship or post-doc or assistant dean's job. In that case, you start to think in terms of finding other employment. The classic case was that of Albert Einstein: "His impudence and lack of deference to authority . . . alienated all of his professors at Zurich Polytechnic . . . he was the only graduate in his section . . . not offered a junior professorship."[6]

His situation made his career. A job was found for him at the Swiss Patent Office that gave him time away from the pressures of meeting classes and grinding out research papers so that he could think. The result was the theory of relativity and much more. Eventually, he was invited to become a professor.

The point of this story is that innovation and creativity can be gained outside an academic career as much as inside. When you achieve the PhD degree, it is a point of discontinuity in your life when many alternative paths are open to you. A tenure track position in the academy is only one of them. But, if you choose academia, then be prepared to teach, even if you have research funding, as you will always be in an environment where you are teaching something to someone. If you are entrepreneurial, the right environment in academia can offer autonomy. Life, after all, is what you make of it.

73. Non-university research organizations offer the challenge of research without the need or the opportunity to teach.
They include industry laboratories, major consulting firms, government laboratories, and nonprofit think tanks. Each organization has its distinct culture. Many involve defense or government work. In the nonprofits and the consulting firms, you are only as good as the last contract you brought in and there is typically a lot of travel. As a result, these organizations experience a high burnout rate among people 45 or older. If you want to go back to academia at some time in the future, you need to create your own portable wealth by publishing. Unfortunately, publishing is counter to the culture of many of these organizations. In some industrial laboratories it is said that if you write $F = ma$ or $E = mc^2$, someone will stamp your report "Company Confidential." That stamp or publishing a report, say in defense, that is marked "Classified," means that you will not be able to include this publication in a tenure dossier.

74. Research versus teaching-oriented institutions.
When job hunting, one of the first choices you make is applying to teaching or to research institutions (typically called R1). The two types differ in that teaching schools require some research output, and research schools require lots of research output. Both require teaching skills.

Your choice depends on whether you think of yourself first as a teacher who does research or as a researcher who also teaches.

Research institutions are typically mega-universities. If your field is part of science, technology, engineering, and mathematics (STEM), or similar areas supported by government and grant organizations, you will be expected to bring in research money to support your research, to be involved in writing grant applications almost from the day you arrive, and also to be involved in the PhD program.

Teaching institutions want you to have a PhD to certify your intellectual ability to do research and also to satisfy accreditation requirements to be credentialed one level above that which you are teaching; however, they may not insist that you are a prolific researcher. Nonetheless, the ability to obtain grants will help you with tenure and promotion. However, do not think that just because you wrote your dissertation that you can write a National Institutes of Health (NIH) grant, for example. They are *very* different.

75. The jobs may be at for-profit institutions.[6] Read Hint 54 before deciding to take a job at a for-profit school. For-profit schools can carry a large amount of baggage that makes them less attractive than nonprofits for an academic job. Fifteen years ago, the significant growth in academia was in the for-profit sector. The argument about lack of growth in nonprofits is by analogy. During that same time period, job growth among businesses five years old or more was zero. Furthermore, almost no nonprofit tenure-granting institutions opened then, nor have they opened since.

Conclusion: Nonprofit higher education is a mature industry. Most of the jobs involve replacing people who leave or retire. Yes there is some regional growth, but it is offset by contraction elsewhere.

76. New programs. Colleges, like businesses, respond to perceived demand when offering new programs. The programs may be a new school (e.g., law, pharmacy, nursing, computing), a new department, or a new area in an existing department. The advantages of such programs are that they are not encumbered by their past, usually have more than one position available, and have a future. However, they are not risk free. Sometimes subjects that seem to be leading edge or potential winners turn out not to be. If few students show up, the programs are canceled, and the people who were hired wind up back in job-hunting mode. If you land such a job, be aware that you will be expected to help set up the curriculum and the necessary infrastructure. That cuts into your research productivity and hence your ability to be hired elsewhere. Bottom line: You need to be careful and be willing to take the risk.

To find new programs, examine the employment ads in the *Chronicle of Higher Education* and the lists of new programs that appear from time to time in *Inside Higher Education*.

77. National rankings. When considering places to send your job application, and if you choose those places based on national rankings of schools and departments, be very careful. Rankings of universities and departments are strongly influenced by a halo effect. In a classic case several years ago, Penn State's law school was ranked well by law school deans, but there was one little problem: Penn State did not have a law school at that time.[7] Since then, some law schools have decided to remove themselves from the rankings process.[8]

Measurement problems that plague, and often invalidate, such rankings include the following:

- In your discipline, a poorly ranked university may have the top-ranked department while that of a leading university may be mediocre.
- Graduate programs, and universities, achieve status almost entirely through scholarly publications (or football teams), not through effective teaching. Graduate department ratings, and by implication overall university ratings, are profoundly affected by institutional and departmental size. There is a strong correlation between department ranking and the total number of articles by its faculty published in highly cited journals. The correlation is much lower when per-faculty publication rates are used. So naive aspiring faculty candidates who apply to departments based on rank may be choosing large departments characterized by low levels of research and poor teaching.

Many institutions try to game or play the system to inflate their quality ratings. They know ranking organizations use variables that are easy to obtain and then the institutions adjust their metrics accordingly. As a newly minted PhD or when changing jobs, you should focus on your fit with a department and on whether the culture is supportive rather than on rankings. The information you really need is given in the other hints in this chapter but is not usually reflected in published rankings.

Nonetheless, ratings for the school as a whole, not the department, affect your reputation and the quality levels of students you wind up teaching. It is also important to understand that not all ratings are created equally. There are many different rating organizations. The most widely known is US News & World Reports which universities and programs cannot "pay to play." Over the last several years, US News & World Reports has reexamined their ranking methodologies. It is important to recognize that changing metrics and methodologies could result in different rankings over the years. There are, however, many other ranking organizations that rank programs and these programs may pay a fee for the evaluation and subsequent posting on their website. Be suspicious if the methodology is not posted on the website or if it is not sound and rigorous. Find out how the university or program is ranked and by whom, but recognize that even if the methodology is posted, it may change and so may the ranking.

78. Teaching in a community college. Doctoral students don't usually envision themselves as being in training for a position in a two-year community college. However, in a tight job market, and with skills in teaching, these institutions are a source of jobs for those completing the doctorate and once that degree is in hand.

Community colleges play an important role in our higher education system. They are engines of social mobility. Many talented students cannot afford to attend a four-year institution right out of high school. They plan to matriculate at their local community college for two years and then transfer. Other students seek advanced vocational or technical training and certification for well-paid jobs in our economy. Some of those students are reverse transfers, people with a bachelor's degree who seek specialized knowledge and skills leading to employment.

The prevalence of community colleges varies from state to state. Depending on where you are located and the state or federal funds earmarked for community college development, a faculty position at a community college actually can pay more than a public four-year college or public universities with graduate programs.

Be aware of the trade-offs. Your teaching load will be heavy. However, the teaching can be challenging and fulfilling. You will not be encouraged to conduct research, but you can discipline yourself to conduct research and publish if your goal is to join a research institution.

79. Online universities. Online universities are proliferating, but they vary in quality. Some are highly questionable and may be perceived as degree mills. Others are well-organized, accredited, respected academic organizations. Some online universities provide extensive training programs for new faculty, including discussion of teaching standards.

80. Teaching overseas for fun and profit. You can become involved in teaching overseas in several ways. Here are a few:

- Your institution runs an overseas program and asks you to teach in it for a semester or a year.
- You are hired specifically by a college to teach overseas.
- You are hired by an institution in another country.
- You receive a Fulbright or other grant that includes overseas teaching.

Advantages: If you're interested in the country or have relatives there, you can visit them with your travel expenses paid, and you can travel within the region at a much lower cost than if you were leaving from the United States as your starting point. If your research involves the country, you can do it there. You can familiarize yourself with foreign cultures and attend overseas conferences. You will develop a broader outlook and make new friends.

Disadvantages: You probably will not be able to do much research while you are abroad. If untenured, you lose time on your tenure clock (Hint 192), unless you can arrange to stop the clock while away. You incur some extra costs (for example, shutting down your home in the United States).

Bottom line: Weigh the benefits and the costs. Investigate the economics involved, and try not to wind up subsidizing the experience.

DATA GATHERING

In addition to gathering data about a potential employer before you submit an application, you will be gathering data during and after the interview to help you decide whether that institution is one you want to be part of.

81. Determine the culture. Peter Drucker said, "Culture eats strategy for lunch." While you want to choose your job strategically, culture is paramount. In large institutions, school and department cultures will differ, ranging from cooperative to cutthroat. Often the culture will change when a new person is appointed president or provost or dean or department chair. That is what makes these appointments so critical to the quality of your life. A cooperative culture should be treasured; it will help you as a young faculty member. But, a cutthroat culture is particularly stressful for young faculty because they arrive not knowing the culture of the place nor being prepared for it. When interviewing, try to find out whether the members of the faculty like one another, and try to assess the cultural norm from what they tell you. Asking graduate students about faculty infighting won't help because they are usually insulated from it. Remember that in addition to trying to assess your capabilities and fit with their needs, the interviewers are trying to present as good a picture of themselves as they can so you will accept their offer should they make one. Thus, always assume that actual conditions are much worse than they are painted during the interview. If you are lucky enough to receive multiple offers, investigate the cultures involved in your choice by speaking to anyone you know at the school and anyone who recently left it.

82. Assessing culture. Develop a set of culture related questions and make sure to ask every person with whom you interview the exact same question. If they all answer the same or similarly, then the culture is likely consistent with the answers. Trust what you are being told.

83. Listen and integrate. Academia and industry have some very different ways of thinking, problem solving, and team work. It is a big learning curve to go from one to the other. When joining a team, it can be disruptive if you do not understand the social dynamics and cultural norms of your team. Take time to silently observe and learn. Then, steadily integrate yourself into conversations and learn how others communicate to help you become persuasive in your communication with them.

84. Gather salary and tenure data. Two pieces of data about an institution that are important to you answer the following questions: Are you being offered the right amount of money? and What are the chances of your achieving tenure (see next hint)? To answer the first question, obtain information on the salary levels for people in your field. The American Association of University Professors publishes salary averages for many (but not all) colleges. Additionally, if you are applying to a public university, most of those have salary data publicly available. You may need to dig for it and there may be a one-year lag. You should make a spreadsheet with all of those in the same department, in same rank as you, their time since degree, and their salary. This will come in handy for negotiation. See Chapter 11 for more on salaries.

85. Obtaining information on tenure decisions is tricky. First, the number of tenure cases per year in an academic unit tends to be small. You need data for your specialty. However, knowing the tenure fraction for the institution as a whole is also important. If a school tenures one in ten, it is a far different place from one that tenures eight in ten. Just knowing the success percentages in the tenure process is not enough. Some schools weed out at the three-year point. Others make tenure so tough that faculty self-destruct by resigning early. Talk with people who recently made tenure in the department; they will usually have the best view of the current situation.

86. Ask about the retirement system. You may think that you are far away from retirement, and you might be, but when you are closer to retirement, you will thank your "now self" for paying attention to this as it can affect your mobility economically from then on. You will most likely be in a state retirement system or in the Teachers Insurance and Annuity Association (TIAA) retirement system. TIAA is subscribed to by most private and some public institutions. In TIAA, once vested (these days, it's usually at once) you keep what you have when you move to another institution. State retirement plans are portable within the state but not from one state to another. The major problem comes when you move from a TIAA college to a state institution or the other way around. Although these funds can be transferred, this needs to be done thoughtfully to avoid tax implications. Do not act hastily, but rather consult with various knowledgeable people about doing so. For more about retirement, see Hint 212.

87. Parking. Be sure to inquire about parking, because parking can be a big deal and is frequently a very hot topic on campuses. For example, at the University of California the joke is that the university is really a parking business that runs its ten campuses as a way to attract customers. Parking is such a hot topic at the University

JOB HUNTING

Hint 87 Be sure to inquire about parking . . .

of Alabama at Birmingham, they ran a phishing campaign around parking and several employees gave up credentials to their accounts! Unless you wind up living a short walk or bike ride from your campus office or living in a city with decent public transportation with stops near your home and your campus, you have little choice but to drive to get to work. If you do, you may be charged a parking fee, usually deducted from your pay. Whether you pay a fee or not, all you get is a hunting license to find a space somewhere. Some schools do offer reserved parking in a specific area at an increased fee, which means that a space is available but not the same one every day. The top fee can be substantial; $750 a year for a reserved space is not uncommon. You can't do much about parking costs except to carpool, walk, ride your bike, or take public transit. But carpooling is difficult because you need to find people who live near you and who are on campus at the same times you are. Be sure to include parking costs in analyzing the true income associated with an offer.

88. Determine "real pay." Don't assume that the only relevant dollar number associated with an offer is the total salary. It isn't. What you most need to know is how much money you can spend, how much the spending money can buy, and the quality of life associated with the offer. Here are some considerations.

- Cost of housing. The cost is greater and house sizes are smaller in, say, Los Angeles, CA than they are in Cedar Falls, Iowa.
- Cost of living other than housing (such as goods and services). College towns and big cities are generally more expensive to live in, but offer more amenities such as theater and cultural and sports activities. Look at gasoline prices and visit a supermarket to do some quick comparisons.
- Quality of schools for your children. Housing sites, such as Zillow, will list school scores. The best method is to ask faculty with children when you interview. They know the ins and outs that sometimes are not reflected in scores.
- Local tax structure for sales, state income, and real estate taxes. Yes, you will make enough money that you need to worry about taxes.
- Availability of work for your spouse in the community. Do not discount the fact that your spouse's company may offer remote work as a compromise to maintain an excellent employee.
- We suggest looking at a cost-of-living calculator before your campus visit. Here is an example of a cost of living calculator from the Economic Research Institute: https://www.erieri.com/cost-of-living-comparison.

OFFERS

89. Get the offer in writing, read it, and negotiate before you accept. Once you are selected by a search committee you usually receive the offer over the phone. The phone conversation usually includes the salary offered, what your title will be, and a few other details. You will be pressed to make a decision quickly (sometimes on the spot), because if you decline, the school will offer the position to its backup candidate. We recommend you find out about the details of the offer and negotiate if necessary before you accept. If this is your first offer, we strongly suggest that you consult with your adviser or a mentor who understands how academia salaries operate. They may be able to help you understand that you cannot get more in salary, but you can increase the amount of the start up package, or negotiate for a high-end computing system.

Get the offer in writing, including all the detailed promises that were made and agreed to. Not only do you want the job, but the institution has decided you are the one, and it wants you badly. Be aware that the administrators who make the offer may, and often do, lie. Their memory loss when you arrive on campus can far exceed anything that could be expected at their stage of life, telling you that there must have been a misunderstanding. As we said, get it in writing.

You will find details about your work life throughout this book, ranging from teaching loads to computing support to research time to parking. Make a list of what is critical for you (don't forget to include items from Chapter 15). Then obtain clarification and agreement in writing about items not in the offer. If things get sticky, the university is technically only bound to uphold what is in the letter and nothing else. That being said, we have seen promises made in emails being used successfully during grievances.

90. Get your PhD before you start the tenure track, unless you are starving or homeless. Don't take a tenure-track faculty position without the PhD in hand. If you do, we estimate the odds are two to one against your ever finishing your degree. Even if you do finish while on the job, your chances of being tenured go down because you reduced the seven-year clock (see Hint 192). Furthermore, without a PhD you will be offered a significantly lower salary, and you may never make up the difference. If you must work, the only defense you have is to negotiate with the institution that the clock does not start ticking until you can legitimately be called Doctor.

91. Avoid taking your first job at a school you attended. Don't do this: No matter how strong your loyalty is, how tempting this is, or how secure your job is. You will always be regarded as a graduate student or staff by the older faculty and will be treated as such. It is different, however, if you leave for some years and then return.

92. Choosing among offers. Your lifestyle is a prime consideration in your job search. Create a table listing what is important to you and how each offer matches your list. You may want to prepare this list (see Hint 89) before you go on the market, as the list provides guidance about what to look for in your job hunt.

Decide which offer comes closest to the way you (and your family) want to live over the many years that follow. Remember, no institution will be perfect.

Just picking the offer with the largest salary is much too simple. The government's consumer price index (CPI) is an indicator of how far the money will go in a particular location. For example, the New York City CPI is high, but transportation is cheap. In Los Angeles the CPI is lower, but you must own a car and have to drive a lot. Housing prices are high in both places but low in rural settings. Make your evaluation in terms of your lifestyle. See Hint 88 for cost comparison information.

Ignore small differences in the salary offered. A $1,000-a-year difference comes down to about $20 a week.

Examine benefits such as health insurance, retirement contributions, and others, for example, travel allowances), computer support, sabbatical leave (Hint 225), and tuition remission for your children or domestic partners. Benefits can be quite different among offers (Hint 88).

Quality-of-life issues also include school systems, airport access, climate, and the availability of your favorite type of entertainment, be it symphony, theater, country dancing, or hunting.

HUNTING FOR THE NEXT JOB

93. Positioning yourself for the next job. Professors, like everyone else, make mistakes. You may find you have great qualms about the job you took and desperately want to get out. It may be that you find the lifestyle suffocating or your colleagues unbearable or the students unprepared for your subject or your significant other desperately is unhappy or the school decides to fire you after three years. Whatever the cause, you want to restart your life in a new institution. In this moment of panic you need to think through what to do with the rest of your life. Here are some suggestions.

- Be discreet. Don't go around telling everyone how bad life is; people are mostly happy and they don't want to hear about it. Certainly don't bad-mouth the institution or leave in a huff. You want to leave amicably so that you receive decent recommendations. Remember, tenured academics have long memories and are around for a considerable time.
- You are back at square one, where you were when you received your PhD. The job-hunting steps are the same:
  - Update your CV and record everything you've accomplished since your degree.
  - Check for advertised available openings. Attend conferences where recruiting occurs.
  - Circulate your CV.

- Tell your mentor(s) and people you know and trust that you would like to move. They know you, and most of them will want to help. They will tip you off about positions that might fit you. If any are considered 1 of the 100 powerful people in the field (Hint 2), so much the better.
- You can be general about your reasons for leaving and couch them in terms of looking for new opportunities. Be aware that even if you try to keep your desire to move quiet, leaks occur, some of which inevitably reach your institution. If you have a boss who believes that even thinking of leaving their Land of Eden is treason, be prepared for trouble.
- It is easier to move to a school that is lower in the pecking order than higher. Administrators at midlevel schools like to brag that they hired from the Ivy League and so on down the line. Horizontal moves do occur sometimes, but only for those with an impressive record.
- The best position is when someone from an institution better or equal to yours approaches you. Unfortunately, that situation is infrequent, even if you have special talents in a hot area.
- Regardless of where you wind up, make sure your offer letter specifically spells out that all work completed before employment at The Next University will count toward tenure and promotion. Otherwise, you are really back at square one.
- Make sure you read the faculty handbook cover to cover at The Next University and especially that you understand the tenure and promotion guidelines. Most universities have policies and procedures around granting tenure and/or promotion at hire.

94. If you become unemployed. People in academia do lose their jobs. They are fired, not tenured, their department is eliminated, or they quit. If it happens to you, you are suddenly back to where were before you received your PhD.

Unemployment is not trivial. You may not be eligible for unemployment insurance. Even if you are, government insurance pays much less than your current salary. You stand to lose benefits, such as health insurance. Unless you are independently wealthy, you need employment, and you need it quickly.

Fortunately, unless you quit on the spur of the moment in a huff in the middle of a semester, you have time between when you know you need a job and when your paycheck stops. Use that time to move back into employment. Here are some things you can do.

- To stay in academia, search the job openings in the *Chronicle of Higher Education* and *Inside Higher Education*. You may have to move to a lower-ranking institution or teach at a for-profit school (Hint 54).
- Consider temporary one-year visiting professor appointments and assistant deanships.

- Accept adjunct teaching appointments in other institutions within traveling distance. We don't recommend adjunct appointments that require moving, unless you are in a small, isolated college town with no local options.
- Complete a book that offers a decent advance against royalties. However, this arrangement is easier said than done.
- Investigate nonprofit and for-profit nonacademic organizations that require skills you have, such as translating a foreign language or knowledge of statistics or finance. Some firms won't touch a PhD (overqualified), while others like the idea of a PhD on their staff.

In many situations you may need to move, which is more difficult if you have a working spouse. If your working spouse has skills useful at a university, see Hint 57.

NOTES

1 None of the authors has ever worked for a for-profit educational organization. Our opinions are based on what we observed over a couple of decades.

2 For the results of this survey, see Tom Harkin, "The Return on the Federal Investment in For-Profit Education: Debt without a Diploma." United State Senate, Health, Education, Labor, and Pensions Committee. https://www.help.senate.gov/imo/media/doc/Education%20Report.pdf. Accessed October 23, 2024.

3 https://en.wikipedia.org/wiki/List_of_for-profit_universities_and_colleges#Closed_or_merged. Accessed June 1.2024.

4 See E. Wolf, "Standing Out from the Herd." *Inside Higher Education,* October 13, 2010. https://www.insidehighered.com/advice/2010/10/13/standing-out-herd. Accessed June 1, 2024.

5 For more details on interview tactics, see T. Wright, "If I Could Do It Over." *Inside Higher Education,* October 27, 2010. https://www.insidehighered.com/advice/2010/10/27/if-i-could-do-it-over. Accessed June 1, 2024.

6 *Los Angeles Times,* April 8, 2007, in a story on Albert Einstein.

7 M. Gladwell, "The Order of Things." *New Yorker,* February 14, 2011, 68–75.

8 https://www.insidehighered.com/admissions/article/2022/11/17/harvard-and-yale-law-will-not-participate-us-news-rankings. Accessed August 11, 2024.

Chapter 5
Teaching and Service

Hint 102 Students are very conscious of the amount of money they spend for your class.

All faculty members, whether at a teaching or a research institution, spend a considerable portion of their lives in the classroom and involved in service that helps govern the institution. Teaching is a fundamental condition for staying in academe. Furthermore, you may find that teaching and mentoring provide some of your most rewarding professional experiences. You have the opportunity to make a positive impact on your students' careers and lives.

95. Publications are the only form of portable wealth. Teaching provides great personal satisfaction and is an important public good that you perform. It is an important, necessary condition but not a sufficient one for being hired or tenured.

96. Many colleges and universities value teaching. Some people want to become professors, they love to teach, and they believe research is a necessary evil to get their ticket punched. Without publishing, it is impossible to receive tenure in most schools, particularly in research universities. Happily, however, the pendulum is swinging. Many colleges and even some universities now value teaching and reward it on its own merits. But you'd better be a super teacher.

97. Teaching is a learned art. As such it follows a learning curve. Your first effort will not be as good as your second, and your second, not as good as your third. However, there is a limit to how good you will get. In other words, your teaching ratings will peak and then remain essentially constant. Eventually, you will be bored by the course, and your teaching ratings will go down. Don't despair. It is a natural phenomenon, often a result of aging. Faculty over 40 relate less and less each year to 18-year-old freshmen if they don't have kids at home any more. Decreasing teaching ratings are a signal that it is time for you to teach a different course or students at a different level. You may need to strong-arm your department chair, but change you must.

98. Be a mentor.[1] Strive to be a good mentor as well as a good teacher. The difference between the two terms is subtle, but important. Mentoring almost always refers to guiding a person in their pursuits—in this case a student getting a degree.

Mentoring is a key component of your responsibilities if you work with PhD students and, to a lesser degree, if you work with master's or undergraduate students. If you do mentoring well, you create friends for life. Years from now you will inevitably conclude that your most important and most personally satisfying professional contributions came from mentoring.

Take the mentoring responsibility seriously. Commit time and energy to guiding your mentees. If you had a helpful mentor, think carefully about how they helped you. In addition to the theories, models, literature, and analytical techniques you impart, take time to help your protégés get over intellectual hurdles, and tell them about the practical aspects of career development. Make students aware of the choices they face and the associated pros and cons. Don't make decisions for them; give them the information they need to make wise choices.

Learn how to improve your teaching and mentoring from the extensive literature about college teaching, teaching in general, and mentoring.

99. Relationships with students. Students are human and so are you . . . and not too long ago, you were a student. Never, ever forget what it was like when you were a student. Students have emotions and can get easily overwhelmed (and so can you as a new faculty member). Listen to your students and offer choices rather than concrete advice. Sometimes, they just want to know that what they are feeling is normal.

100. Be relatable. If your students tell you they are overwhelmed, understand and appreciate the level of vulnerability that this took to tell you—be a good listener. Don't be afraid to show your own vulnerabilities to students—faculty do not need to be omnipotent—they need to be human. These relationships can last a lifetime, but understand that some will not. It is OK to have students that drive you nuts—use this as a good learning opportunity and reflect that you might have been the same way as a student.

101. Go to Toastmasters International. If you need tips on how to be entertaining and informative in front of a group of students, Toastmasters International is an excellent worldwide organization to get some experience (www.toastmasters.org). We have seen it work in many cases. Ignore the fact that Toastmasters attracts mostly business people; the environment gives you privacy from your colleagues.

102. Meeting classes is paramount. Don't cancel classes. For example, if you are out of town attending a national scholarly meeting on a class day, arrange for a colleague to cover for you or arrange a makeup time with the class. If you know far enough in advance when you will be out of town, you can schedule an examination on that day, and be sure it is proctored properly. Missing classes creates more ill will from students than anything else you do. If you miss a lot of classes, even if they are covered by someone else, students will resent it. Students assume they are taking the class from you, not from a collection of substitutes. In high-tuition institutions (and even in some modest ones) students are very conscious of the amount of money they spend for your class. They will take it out on you on your class ratings and complain to the department chair and your colleagues. In addition, you will pile up debts to colleagues you must repay by covering their classes for them. If you have to repay many such debts, you will lose valuable time from your research and thus from your tenure clock.

103. Academia and campus safety. It doesn't happen very often, but a student can come into your office or your building and shoot at you or cause other physical harm. The 2007 tragedy at Virginia Tech, where a student shot and killed 33 people including himself, is a poignant example, and unfortunately there are many other examples like this. As the political climate becomes increasingly heated and world peace seems unachievable, campuses have become proving grounds with oftentimes less than peaceful demonstrations. While academia itself is not an unsafe profession, the campus, where free speech is encouraged, can become an unsafe *environment* when protests take a wild turn or someone is triggered over something unknown, such as a bad grade. As stated in Hint 227, as a faculty member you are a public person; your actions affect the lives of real people. Students (and your colleagues, for that matter) are prone to the same mental disturbances as people in society as a whole. A few may be sufficiently unbalanced to take harmful action.

You can reduce your risk by learning about aberrant behavior (e.g., talk to the psychology staff at your campus health service) and by reporting your concerns to the health service or campus police. Be aware of your campus's policy and don't try to solve the problem on your own. You may become a target.

104. Consider costs to students when selecting textbooks. In general, the least considered factor that goes into the selection of a text for a course is its cost. Admittedly, you have no choice when teaching one or more sections of a standard multi-section course whose text is selected by a committee or a course coordinator. However, when you alone make the choice, cost should be one of the criteria in your selection.

105. Avoid serving on a committee where you are the technical expert. If you know something about libraries, don't serve on the library committee. If you do, you will be put in the subgroup (or worse, become the subgroup) to make recommendations or solve the mess in your area of expertise, and that will eat up enormous amounts of your time with little visible results and even less personal gain for you.

IN THE CLASSROOM[2]

106. Summaries lock in the material. Save time at the end of a lecture for a clear, succinct summary of what you presented. Ask yourself, "What key points do you want your students to remember?" Similarly, begin each class with a clear, short summary of what you presented in the previous session. At times, the short-term memory of distracted students (Hint 121) is as unreliable as that of some senior citizens. They need to be reminded what happened on Tuesday.

107. Encourage questions. Establish ground rules about questions. The students should ask them when they have them, not wait silently for 15 minutes until it is "question time." If a student is confused by a concept, they will become totally lost in a subsequent discussion that builds on that concept, unless you clarify it right then. However, students also should raise their hand when they have a question and wait for you to call on them. Do not answer questions that are shouted out, especially, "What did you just say?" Of course, if the students do that often enough they're telling you that your voice or their hearing is going.

108. Enjoy your classes. Presumably, you selected your field because you find it interesting and enjoyable. Many students accept that they should, or must, master your subject, such as statistics or opera, but consider it odious. Make the material come alive for them the way it does for you. You can teach statistics with gambling examples. The plots for the great operas make soap operas and police dramas look tame by comparison. One colleague encountered high school students who said they hated math. "You like money, don't you?" he asked. "Of course," they replied. "Well, making money is all about math. Let me show you how."

109. Lecturing versus facilitating. Faculty who spend their class time lecturing and faculty who prefer facilitating appear to be in a constant state of tension. In the classical model of lecturing the faculty member walks into the classroom, opens the textbook or sets up the PowerPoint, and proceeds to drone on until the bell mercifully rings or the prepared material ends so the class can be dismissed early. This rigid scenario does not create a positive learning environment.

Before discussing how to lecture, it is worth asking why lecture at all? We contend that the course in which pure lecture or pure facilitation is the right approach is rare. Most undergraduate and graduate students don't know enough about a course's subject when they attend its first meeting to be able to discuss much more than what they saw on their social network or looked up on Wikipedia. They haven't read the textbook or the literature, and they don't know what the issues are or even why some ideas are issues at all.

110. Teaching is not synonymous with lecturing. Increasingly, professors are encouraged to be the "guide on the side" and not the "sage on the stage." A growing body of literature deals with ways to engage students and to facilitate their learning above and beyond the traditional lecture, including class discussions and group projects. Try some of these other modes of teaching, and read about innovative pedagogical strategies.

Find an effective combination of strategies that seems to work for you. The approaches you select have to work for your personality. Furthermore, the relative value of a lecture versus, say, group discussion varies by discipline.

111. Flipping the learning. Commonly called a flipped classroom, this is an instructional strategy that inverts the traditional teaching model. In the flipped classroom, students are encouraged to learn new content outside the classroom and then bring that into the classroom. This works especially well in graduate education where it is expected that students are in control of their own learning as they hone their higher-order thinking skills (i.e. critical thinking and problem solving). Try breaking your semester into several bigger concepts and then have students "teach" some sections to the rest of the class . . . and to you. Be careful not to abdicate your responsibilities—students do not like this. While you act primarily as a facilitator in this environment, we bet that you will learn a lot in the process, and this becomes more enjoyable for everyone.

112. Lecture capture. The electronic gizmos being sold to help teaching at the college level keep increasing, with one or two important new gadgets seeming to pop up every year. In 2011, as we wrote the second edition, electronic lecture capture was the rage. Electronic lecture capture refers to recording lectures or class discussions so students can watch the lecture at their convenience on their own computer or at the library. During the COVID-19 pandemic, Zoom became widely used, almost universal. Lectures on Zoom can easily be recorded. Most of the time, this is done via a platform like Canvas, which means that only students registered for the course can view your lecture. But there are alternative platforms through which your lectures may be made public.

Whether lecture capture improves learning remains to be determined. Whether lecture capture will be used to increase class sizes, reduce the number of faculty required, or reduce most students to essentially taking courses online even though they are registered for face-to-face classes is not known.

The following are important questions for prospective and young faculty:

- Who owns the lecture's intellectual property? With lecture capture you can be cloned many times over (or even sold to other institutions) and receive nothing for the residual rights, as they are called in the entertainment business.
- What is the potential payoff for you? Your reputation could grow as a wider range of students view your lectures and are impressed by them.

113. Presentation software. PowerPoint and other presentation software are powerful visual complements to lecturing. The software is user-friendly, visuals are easy to create, and students are accustomed to it. Presentations are most powerful when the text is sparse and primarily serves as a reminder.

Putting detailed information in your presentations loses your audience. They will not be listening to you because, after studying the display, they will spend their time copying the text in their notebooks. If you simply read what is on your presentation, the students will tune you out.

Prepare hard-copy versions of your presentation images (typically six to a page) for distribution. They serve as a backup if the technology fails, and if the technology works perfectly, hand out the hard copies after your lecture. Otherwise, you may find yourself talking to the tops of their heads as they study the papers in front of them. For students, the hard copy serves as a record, consulted at exam time. Just go to a school cafeteria before an exam and you will find students studying the handouts or using them to test one another.

If you are dissatisfied with PowerPoint, alternative presentation software is available on the market.

TEACHING ONLINE

114. Digital natives versus digital immigrants. Digital natives, a term coined in 2001 by Marc Presky, a writer on education, refers to those born after 1985 and who have grown up with technology—these are our students. Many faculty are digital immigrants, meaning that they were not born into a technology world, but rather adopted it later. The digital natives are now wearing their email and their phone on their wrist (integrated with their smartwatch) and can look up information before the professor has a chance to finish explaining it. This has changed and will continue to change everything from how we teach, to how we grade, to how we interact. Now . . . enter artificial intelligence (AI). Simply put, digital natives think differently.

115. Distance education. Distance education does not necessarily involve distance, but rather refers to courses offered over the Internet to students in other locations rather than in face-to-face classroom settings. The earliest such courses used television transmission of live classes to people in local industry. Remote students could respond and ask questions via a voice link. Today these courses use the Internet, are referred to as online, and they range from audio courses available on demand to courses at fixed times with instructors present to two-way video conferencing. The greater the richness of the medium, the greater the cost. Online instruction is an increasing option for students.

Online is a much more intense way of teaching. It can require:

- More time to prepare
- More time in individual student contacts (often around the clock because they can be overseas)
- Dealing with a broader range of student skills and maturity
- Good to excellent Internet skills
- Great patience

To understand what is involved with teaching online, talk with experienced faculty at your institution and observe one or more of their classes.

116. Distance learning is a blessing and a threat. It is a blessing because you can reach students who would otherwise not have the opportunity to learn from you or to savor the beauties of your field. It is a threat because administrators of colleges and universities might learn that it is cheaper to buy the infrastructure for distance learning than to construct new buildings or to hire new faculty. With distance learning you can instruct (some would say distract) hundreds simultaneously, not just the 10 or 30 in your classroom. Also, if you are not a super teacher on video or the Internet, you may not find much of a future market for your services, even if you are a great researcher.

STUDENTS

117. Be wary of student excuses. The death rate among aunts and grandmothers of college-age students is phenomenal, far beyond actuarial reality, and it increases as exam time approaches. Although some students are remarkably inventive at concocting stories for this standard excuse for missing classes and exams, most are not. Faced with such an excuse, be aware that the student may be working you. These excuses can also snowball: If one student gets away with it, others follow, and you face a veritable epidemic of death among your student's relatives.

118. Believe it or not, cheating is widespread at some institutions. If you give tests, we suggest setting up the testing environment so that the test questions automatically rotate. This way, each student gets a different question at a different time.

119. Teach every student. As an educator, your goal should be to lead each and every student to master your subject.

Do not approach your work with the attitude that the material is difficult, only a few of them are intelligent enough to understand it, and you can't be concerned with the rest.

Don't assume that some students cannot learn the material, even advanced technical content, because they lack the aptitude or intelligence. Such judgments almost always are incorrect. Furthermore, they create a destructive self-fulfilling prophecy. If you believe that women can't learn advanced multivariate statistics (which is incorrect), or that a certain student is just not smart enough, that will color your instruction, your reactions to the student's questions or comments, and your evaluations of their work.

120. Teach to the student's frame of reference. Learn as much as you can about each student's prior educational experiences, particularly in your discipline; their work experience; and hobbies or leisure interests. Consider asking about their educational and professional experience in a carefully structured first assignment (but stop short of asking intrusive personal questions).

Later, try to frame answers to a student's questions with metaphors and examples they can relate to. For a nurse or nursing student, use medical metaphors. For an athlete, use sports metaphors. For a political science major, use examples from politics, say, in another country. Local or national politics in the United States can be tricky, because the student's political views may be very different from yours.

By learning from the experiences and perspectives your students bring to the table, you will enrich your own understanding of your field.

121. Distracted students. As a new instructor, you will expect to see a sea of eager faces of students who listen to your every word and take copious notes. You may be surprised. You will see students dunking doughnuts and reading the campus newspaper or talking to each other or fondling each other or zoned out listening to their iPods. And what are they really watching on their laptops? Remember, your students, like you, grew up watching television. They forget that you can see them.

What to do about laptops and earbuds ("airpods")? Our advice is laptops during lectures are acceptable. Earbuds and zoning out to music that block out the lecture are not acceptable. Furthermore, we recommend banning laptops and cell phones during tests. It's too easy to communicate about the test via email or texting, and cell phones can be used to photograph the test.

122. Undergraduates don't recall much from seven or more years ago. We all use stories from our past to make a point in class. The stories humanize the material and increase student interest. However, if the stories are too old, traditional-age undergraduates won't know what you're talking about. Examples are movies, books, references to events (particularly events abroad), old computer technologies, or software. If it happened seven or more years ago, it is beyond their recollections. The period of recall is a little longer for older students and graduate students.

123. Will this be on the final? Many students, especially undergraduates, are totally focused on their grades and maximizing their grade point averages (GPAs). They are grade grubbing, and such students measure themselves by the grades they receive. They see themselves as being worth more than you think or more than others think of them. Be it a failing student who thinks he deserves a B, or an A minus student who doesn't understand why she didn't receive at least an A if not an A plus, the story is almost always the same, "You don't see true worth when it is in front of you" and "I worked so hard in this course and was there every day, so I deserve an A." What they don't see is that the grade is a measure of output, not input. All they know about is their own work. You know what they produced in writing or said in class. The stories can be plaintive and even heart wrenching. Don't cave. The word will spread and the cases will multiply.

A key grade grubbing indicator shows up on the first day of class. We are very specific on what different parts of a course are worth, and we include that information in the syllabus. We identify grade grubbers by the inordinate number of questions they ask about something simple in the syllabus, and when these very students receive disappointing test or assignment grades, they swear they never saw the rules in the syllabus.

If you said, "As I was walking from the parking lot to the classroom, I passed a burning bush. A voice from above spoke to me and told me the meaning of life," a student in the front row would surely ask, "Will this be on the final?"

Of course, students never ask you to reduce their grade.

124. Grade inflation. US undergraduate grades have risen substantially over the last six decades, particularly at selective and private colleges.[3] Although the data are clear, their causes are in dispute. Is it because faculty fear student evaluations? Do faculty want to give good students a leg up in graduate school admissions? Does grade inflation in high schools lead students to expect better grades in college? Are adjuncts giving higher grades so they don't lose their jobs? Are today's students really better prepared?

The data imply that you should find out (before your first semester if possible) the current grading norms in your new institution. Don't be too tough, and don't become known as an easy grader. Either reputation hurts you. Award the grades you believe each student earned.

125. Keep up with technobabble. For many, the latest technical jargon, especially when some terms also have conventional meanings, is as impenetrable as the names of hard rock groups are to a devotee of classical music. The terms all sound like technobabble, just as Freudian terms once sounded like psychobabble. Technobabble is what your students know, how they talk, how they write, and how they think. You may even learn words from them that you can use in teaching.

One of us developed a strategy for participating in a conversation with his children and grandchildren about contemporary rock groups. Since all the group names they mention sound totally unfamiliar, he makes up group names: "Have you heard the latest from Broken Promises?" or "Are you a fan of Speed Bumps?"

126. Wikipedia and other Web sources.[4] When you assign students a topic for a paper or ask them to find facts that are new to them, you have to think about Wikipedia and other Web sources. In some faculties, an ever-declining number of Luddite professors argue that Western civilization will inexorably decline if you allow any use of the Web. Such arguments are futile, because students will use these easily available sources as they sit in front of their computers in the middle of the night to prepare the next morning's homework.

You need to get across to students that Wikipedia (like other encyclopedias) does not go into the depth you want your students to go into when researching a topic. Yes, the Wikipedia entries are clear, relevant, organized, contain the basic facts, and provide a broad overview. The entries get students started, but topics explored in sufficient depth and breadth for the typical assignment are few and far between.

You can do two things to wean students from Wikipedia:

- If your students are freshmen or sophomores, few have spent much time in your school's library. Take them there on a field trip and ask the librarians to explain to the students what they can find there, including special collections in your field. Have them do an assignment evaluating Wikipedia in your subject. You could ask them something like, "How good is Wikipedia about Topic A?" or "Is Wikipedia useless?"
- Warn your students that you can catch plagiarism when they copy part of a Wikipedia entry.

127. Letters of reference for students. The time will come when you are asked to write letters of reference for your students to help them obtain a job or get into graduate school. Requests will come from students you treasure and from students you barely remember or whose name and face you couldn't put together on a bet. A simple "Jane Jones attended my class last spring and received an A minus" won't do. You should personalize as much as you can. Ask for a résumé if the student has one. We sometimes find it useful to ask the student to write a draft we can start from, which is a win-win situation and a teaching moment. The students think about how they want to present themselves, something few students do on their own. Even better, you are saved from composing a completely personalized letter from scratch. You save time, and you write a better letter of reference.

128. The student as customer mantra. If you talk to faculty in business or economics you hear this repeatedly: The student is the customer. The corollary is industry's view: The customer is king. Using the language of industry, the customer should have control over the product. In educational terms, it implies that the students should be given more say over what is taught, how it is taught, and how students are judged. Students love this viewpoint, but faculty do not.

Yes, tuition is paid by students, parents, and the school's scholarship funds. But that doesn't make students customers in the same sense as shopping at

Amazon. Most students, particularly graduate students, are motivated and intelligent people making an investment to improve their quality of life.

Students commit to their bachelor's, master's, or PhD education in chunks. It is difficult to switch schools, because credits do not always transfer, requirements differ, and total time to degree increases. In short, once they commit to a school, students are usually stuck until they obtain a degree.

Students do have some influence. For example, over 40 years ago, schools introduced teaching evaluations, and students responded by asking for better facilities, fewer Friday classes, and grade inflation. They rarely ask for more intellectual content. When one business administration dean was asked by a student whether he considered him a customer, the dean replied: "Let's get this straight. You may be paying tuition, but the recruiting companies are the customers—you are merely the product."

129. Be student focused. End every lecture early, even if by a minute or two, and never, ever, go over. Students value talking with faculty one-on-one—be generous with office hours. When there is a choice between making an accommodation for a student or not, make the accommodation, even if it means extending it to the rest of the class (e.g. extending deadlines). Care about your students (see Hint 99).

130. FERPA (Family Educational Rights and Privacy Act). FERPA offers privacy and protections to students and their educational records. While there are some exceptions to FERPA, the general rule is do not disclose anything about a student or their family to anyone. This includes discussing student performance, student hardships, etc. There are five FERPA identifiers that are to be protected. They are:

- The student's name
- The name of the student's parent or other family members
- The address of the student or student's family
- A personal identifier, such as the student's social security number, student number, or biometric record
- Other indirect identifiers, such as the student's date of birth

NOTES

1 We consider writing this book to be a form of mentoring from a distance. Excellent sources on mentoring include these instructive and highly inspirational books: J. Nakamura, D. J. Shernoff, and C. H. Hooker, *Good Mentoring: Fostering Excellent Practice in Higher Education* (San Francisco, CA: Jossey-Bass, 2009); P. Palmer, *The Courage to Teach* (San Francisco, CA: Jossey-Bass, 2007); J. Parini, *The Art of Teaching* (New York, NY:

Oxford University Press, 2005); S. Strogatz, *The Calculus of Friendship: What a Teacher and a Student Learned About Life While Corresponding About Math* (Princeton, NJ: Princeton University, 2011).

2 This section was inspired by Bob Weir's "10 Commandments of Lecturing." *Inside Higher Education*, March 20, 2009. www.insidehighered.com/advice/instant_mentor/weir3

3 S. Roistacher and C. Healy, "Where A is ordinary: The Evolution of American College and University Grading, 1940–2009." *Teachers College Record*, 114(7): 1–23. https://doi.org/10.1177/016146811211400707

4 R. Weir, "Does Wikipedia Suck?" *Inside Higher Education,* March 26, 2010. https://www.insidehighered.com/advice/2010/03/26/does-wikipedia-suck. Accessed August 11, 2024.

Chapter 6
Research

Hint 134 Learn grantsmanship. Don't be snobbish!

RESEARCH

Whether you are affiliated with a research or a teaching institution, you will want to keep up your research. As we said in Hint 95, teaching is a great personal satisfaction, but research productivity is your prime form of portable wealth.

Doing research is a lot easier if you receive a grant from your institution or from an outside source. Unfortunately, most novice faculty have no idea how to obtain grants and are not taught this skill in graduate school. Therefore, we include seven hints on grantsmanship in this chapter as well as hints about research.

131. If you want a research career, make sure the position you are offered allows you to actually do research. If at all possible, negotiate in advance with your future department chair and dean about the conditions of your work. Ask for reduced teaching loads and committee assignments in your first years, seed money for research expenses until you get your grants, equipment (particularly computing equipment), graduate assistants, and more. In particular, obtain a guarantee that you will teach the same courses for the first few years. Your teaching ratings will be better, and you will not divert your energies from research by preparing new courses. Since many of these requests soak up scarce resources, get them written into your offer letter. If you start out without them, it is highly unlikely you will get them later. Even in a tough job market, most of the goodies can be negotiated. Once you are selected, especially if you are the first choice, the department is just as hot for you as you are for it.

132. You can trade off teaching loads and research opportunities. The terms themselves speak volumes about the priorities in many leading universities where, unfortunately, committed and effective teaching is low in status. If you do little research, you will not be tenured in a research (i.e., publish or perish) institution. If you do even a little research in some teaching institutions, it may be held against you; certainly, if you do a lot of research it will not be considered a good thing, especially if it is at the expense of teaching. You can tell what kind of institution you are dealing with by examining the teaching load. Four or five three-unit classes every semester leave most people so exhausted they do not have the energy to do research on any reasonable time scale. These faculty truly carry a load. In a research institution, faculty typically teach two or three courses a semester and are encouraged to obtain outside funding to support their research activities and to reduce their teaching loads. (Be aware that, depending on your contract, if you use research funds to reduce teaching time [i.e. "effort"], this money goes to the school as salary off-set. If you are on a nine- or ten-month contract and you use the money for "summer salary," you will see the money in your summer paycheck).

If you intend to do research, identify opportunities. Life will only get busier. If you think that you can wait until you are less busy to attend to an opportunity, you might find it gone. In graduate school, you likely will not learn all that is necessary to identify funding opportunities and build your "business" within the academic environment. But, you did learn good investigative and inquiry skills.

Use those investigative skills. Just because you are no longer in graduate school does not mean that you stop learning or using key skills like problem solving and resource hunting. Relationship building is key in identifying opportunities.

133. Research requires quantitative and qualitative skills, each of which provides different kinds of insights. Be aware that many qualitative researchers consider quantitative types to be mindless empiricists who fail to grasp the subtleties and nuances of the human experience. And many quantitative researchers believe that all true science is quantitative and, furthermore, that qualitative researchers just aren't smart enough to master mathematical techniques. Both these attitudes are ridiculous.

Regardless of your own research style, master qualitative and quantitative methods. If you don't, a Neanderthal on the tenure committee could cast a negative vote.

134. Learn grantsmanship; it is a skill like any other. If necessary, attend special workshops. Educate yourself about who funds your type of research. Don't be snobbish! You may feel deep down that you did not train yourself for a life of the mind to become a peddler of slick prose to federal and foundation bureaucrats. But an ability to raise money can have a seismic effect on your career. Simply imagine yourself as one of two finalists for the plum academic position you always dreamed about. Your competitor has a $600,000 grant and you don't. What are the odds in your favor?

135. Don't be modest when writing a grant proposal. Present the potential contribution of your proposal in the best possible light.

Keep the budget small or at least reasonable. Remember that funding agencies like sure things, not risks. They'll give a little money to an unknown, but for a large amount they'll want 1 of the powerful 100 (Hint 2) with a track record as a security blanket.

Provide more details than you think necessary about the procedures you will follow. Your friends and colleagues know you are skilled at routine procedures, such as questionnaire surveys or statistical analysis, but a skeptical reviewer who has never heard of you needs to be reassured.

136. Proposal budgets. Your grant proposal is likely your first chance to determine and justify a budget. If you are awarded, then you get to manage a budget. Regardless of whether you are managing your own grant budget or that of a department or school, nothing can short-circuit your grants or management career like a budget deficit. Even if you have a special assistant who is responsible for the budget, you should understand how budgets work. And you should become intimately familiar with the budget of your organization. Otherwise, that budget person will be making the key decisions . . . for you, not with you.

RESEARCH

137. Protest if your brilliant grant proposal is declined. Foundations never use the word *rejected*. Tell the agency that you understand its funds are limited and explain why the research is valuable. It will not change the decision; however, it may pave the way for you to resubmit the idea in the next fiscal year or for you to get favorable treatment on the next submission.

If your proposal is declined, ask if you can have a copy of the reviews. Of course, this requires a thick skin, but you may learn how you can strengthen the proposal for the next time around.

138. Build an advisory panel of nationally respected experts in your grant proposal.[1] Your proposal will then be a little more likely to be funded. If it is, you will benefit from the advice of the experts, and you will expand your network among the top people in the field. Be careful, however. If a national leader agrees to be listed and three or more of your proposals are declined, they may conclude you are a loser. Shuffle the panels from proposal to proposal.

139. If you didn't build in an advisory panel, it's not too late. If you get the grant, it is not too late to create one to achieve visibility. Once funded, invite some of the leading people in your field to participate on your advisory panel (Hint 2). Often you can get them to consult in this way for free or for modest stipends, certainly much less than their outside consulting fee. Your work will benefit from their experience and knowledge, and your visibility will increase significantly.

140. Get the grant approval in writing. Don't count on a grant or contract until you receive the signed letter of approval. (Some people say you should wait until you've cashed the first check.) Some government and foundation officials enthusiastically encourage ideas they later decline. They will blame the change, sometimes appropriately, on their external reviewers or on their advisory committee. Don't believe them until they sign, even if they guarantee funding for the project. It is also important to remember that things change. A five-year grant that was funded in June of an election year could be yanked the following June. Organizations, even the federal government, change their priorities or wind up with less spendable money than originally anticipated.

141. Get clearance before you study an organization. If your research (or that of your students) involves an organization, especially if it involves interviews with its employees, be sure to get clearance for your work before you start, not after completion. No matter how trivial a statement may seem to you, administrators of organizations—private, nonprofit, governmental, or educational—are extremely sensitive about what is said about them. Their public relations groups and their army of lawyers see negative publicity even where no one else does. You risk a lawsuit (and so does your school) if you proceed without their clearance.

Even with clearance before you start, they may insist on reviewing the results and can come back and say no. Everyone is in the public relations game these days.

Consider the following:

- Include a letter of support from the organization with your proposal.
- Run the approved Institutional Review Board (IRB) letter by leadership at the organization.
- Clearance from the organization is needed, even if you have institutional review board clearance (Hint 142).

142. Which brings us to the IRB. The IRB performs critical human subject oversight on scientific, ethical, and regulatory issues, particularly for behavioral and biomedical research. IRBs can be legal, and/or risk mitigation, committees with institution-wide representation that approve, monitor, and review all research involving humans. Creating an IRB application that aligns with the ethical principles outlined in the Declaration of Helsinki requires clear and precise wording. The Declaration of Helsinki, developed by the World Medical Association, provides ethical guidelines for conducting medical research involving human subjects.

You must obtain approval from your IRB before you start your research and before you make any changes to your research protocol. In many programs, you need IRB approval before submitting your dissertation proposal. The IRB also sets time limits on how long their approval is valid. If your research project takes longer than forecast, you must obtain a renewal.

Take IRB seriously as you will likely need to complete an ethics section in your manuscript. In that section, you will have to indicate which IRB sanctioned your study. For example, "This study was conducted under IRB #12343 by the University of _____," or "This study was determined to be 'not human subjects research' by the IRB at the University of _____." IRB traditionally is not needed for quality or process improvement projects. We strongly recommend that you submit your study to the IRB and let them adjudicate the decision.

As you plan your research, explore the characteristics of your university IRB. What do its members look for? What don't they like? The more you know about them before you present your plans, the better off you will be. More often than not, they are consultative and not punitive.

We recommend you take a nationally respected online workshop to learn about IRB issues. Most universities use the Collaborative Institutional Training Initiative (CITI) course training and refreshers are required regularly. It only takes a couple of hours and will answer most of your questions about the IRB and human subjects' research. After completing the course and passing a simple test, you receive a certificate and an ID number. Many governmental organizations require you to present this certificate.

RESEARCH

143. Academic trade journals are sources of higher education (and job) information. Trade journals are published for almost all fields including higher education. The two leading ones are the *Chronicle of Higher Education* and *Inside Higher Education*. The *Chronicle* is a weekly publication, with daily online summaries, containing a broader range of information and tends to be more traditional than *Inside Higher Education*. The *Chronicle* in paper and digital form is expensive, while the much smaller *Inside Higher Education* is a free e-journal that shows up in your email every morning. Both contain job information at no cost. The *Chronicle's* job information, which is free on the Internet, serves as a publication of record for equal employment opportunities and hence has the largest number of listings.[2] *Inside Higher Education* tends to have a narrower range of jobs.

144. Collaborate and cooperate. You are not alone either as a graduate student or as a young faculty member. You collaborate and cooperate with many others. Even the dissertation is not a one-person effort because you work with an adviser and a committee, with people you study if your work involves human subjects (Hint 142) and you interact with fellow graduate students while working on your dissertation. When you begin your academic career, do not tuck yourself away in a corner and try to do it all by yourself. You can collaborate and cooperate with peers, senior faculty, and even students.

In a research institution, you will collaborate on projects with coauthors. Most of them will be close by, but others are from your doctoral program or people you know through conferences (Hint 275) and other professional meetings. Your teaching assistants and your students will help you with specific tasks, including routine ones. You become part of an ongoing group that cooperates on projects, reads and critiques each other's papers before submission, gives you ideas, and receives ideas from you. It is a two-way relationship you need to cultivate.

145. Plagiarism is forbidden. This includes, but is not limited to, using generative AI, such as ChatGPT or other similar tools, to write your text for you. Plagiarism is a form of cheating, which your students may be tempted to try. But you may also wittingly or unwittingly commit plagiarism, particularly in research papers or books. Plagiarism is defined by the Institute for Operations Research and the Management Sciences, which publishes many A-list journals, as "copying of ideas, text, data and other creative work (e.g. tables, figures and graphs) and presenting it as your original work without proper citation."[3]

You need to know and observe the following:

- You *cannot* claim the ideas of others as yours, whether or not you express them in the same way as your source.
- If you copy word for word, you must identify the source and you must put the copied material in quotation marks or, if long, in an indented paragraph.

67

- Be very careful of self-plagiarism, i.e. copying your work from one published source to another published source. If you signed away the copyright in return for being published, you *must* obtain permission of the copyright holder even though you wrote the book or article yourself. For more on self-plagiarism see Hint 153.
- The legal limits on how long a quotation can be are relatively vague. If in doubt, get permission. You (or preferably your institution) may have to pay for permission to quote.

146. Generative AI. When we started revising this book, generative AI (GAI) was just poking its head into academia. Now that we are almost finished with the revision, GAI is in full force in and out of the classroom. It is essential that you understand the strengths of GAI—what it can and cannot do. Students are going to use it (and you should too—it can really help finesse a letter of recommendation). You should understand your university's policy on the use of GAI in the classroom. One of us feels that GAI is fine to use *as a guide* and it must be cited. There must be ethical use of GAI and there must be human-generated quality control. Whatever you decide, it is essential that the degree of use of GAI for course assignments must be addressed in the syllabus.

147. Back up, back up, back up your research (actually everything!). Don't be victimized by unexpected electronic failures that could destroy your files. Always back up important electronic files, including your raw data and the draft text of your research. Keep in mind that research data must be kept for seven years. If your university uses something like Microsoft Office, they likely do nightly back-ups of all work. At 2am when a storm hits and knocks out your files, you cannot rely on that back-up retrieval being expeditious. We recommend that you do your own form of back up, such as on a cloud service like DropBox, Google Drive, or some other external drive that can be easily and readily accessed from anywhere.

Similarly, keep all valuable devices (including computers and removable media) that hold important valuable information secure from theft. Do not assume that theft won't occur in the ivory tower or when you travel. We will spare you the horror stories we have heard. We suggest using a laptop and a docking station so that you take your laptop home with you every night. This still does not mean that your laptop won't get stolen or lost, but it sure makes your work much more portable.

148. Many who earn a PhD never publish anything beyond their dissertation; others publish only one article from the dissertation. If you count how many manuscripts people actually publish, more publish none or one than any other number. Research also shows that if you publish something while in graduate school, you are much more likely to keep publishing after you finish. If you are a researcher, be thankful for this statistic. It reduces the competition for the limited number of articles a journal can publish in an issue. If you are a teacher, take solace in these modal values because they show that many other people, like you, value the art of teaching over research.

NOTES

1 Major think tanks, for example, maintain rosters of such experts, including Nobel Prize winners, who agree to be available for such panels.

2 The link for the *Chronicle*'s jobs page is http://chronicle.com/section/Jobs/61

3 Institute for Operations Research and the Management Sciences, *Guidelines for Plagiarism*, October 21, 2009.

Chapter 7
On Writing

Hint 149 Learn how to write clearly.

Teaching, research, and writing are the three activities academics engage in most. Writing manuscripts— research papers, books, or class notes— requires specialized skills. Here are some thoughts about writing. Publishing what you write is discussed in Chapter 8.

149. Learn how to write clearly. Some graduate programs do their best to stamp out this skill, persuading doctoral candidates that a ten-syllable word is better than a two-syllable word. Reviewers are more likely to persevere to the end of your journal submission or your grant proposal if they can easily follow what you say. They are also more likely to give you a favorable review. If all else fails, use the style of these hints and the writing tips in Appendix D.

150. Learn the fine points of English. With multiple degrees in hand, you are assumed to be an educated person. Writing and speaking mistakes turn off your students, reviewers, and editors of journals.

If you need help, buy *Pocket Fowler's Modern English Usage* and William Strunk Jr. and E. B. White's *The Elements of Style*.[1] Read them. When in doubt, consult them. A well-written article is more likely to be accepted than a poorly written one.

For example, you should:

- Know the difference between *assure*, *ensure*, and *insure*, and between *affect* and *effect*
- Recognize that *criteria* is plural and *criterion* is singular
- Know that the syntax for data is plural and the syntax for datum is singular, so "data were gathered" not "data was gathered." When in doubt, replace the word *data* with the word *they* and you will always use the correct syntax (you would not say *they* was).

To help you with your writing, Appendix D presents a series of simple hints to make your prose sparkle. Absorb them now and go back to them when you finish a draft for submission and apply the principles as you edit the manuscript.

151. Be sure to spell-check, grammar-check, and fact-check your work. Your degrees certify you as a literate, educated person. Grammatical or spelling errors in a CV or in an article submitted for publication turn off reviewers who are making judgments about you. For example, in a CV sent to one of us as an outside reviewer for tenure we found the following: "My research activities has centered on . . . " and a reference to the journal *Group Decision and Negotiation* wound up as *Group Decision & Negation*. Make sure to use spell check critically—it does not always understand the context or what you are actually trying to spell.

152. Editing your own material. As you write your dissertation or paper it is natural to make changes and major revisions. You are, in effect, editing your own material. That's both good and bad. It is good because you add intellectual capital, you clarify, and you consider the knowledge (or lack thereof) of your readers. It is bad if, like most of us, you become infatuated with the sound of your own words. It is difficult, if not impossible, to change language or ideas you labored over long and hard. Additionally, because you wrote it, your brain will automatically fill in words that do not exist or read words correctly that are incorrect.

Just like job application letters, have at least one person (preferably more) read what you wrote and suggest improvements. If a word, a paragraph, or a section is unclear to any of them it is likely to be unclear to others. It's better to receive critiques and suggested improvements from your peers than from referees or decision-makers. Absent someone else to read your work, we suggest putting it aside and not looking at it for a week, then reading it again with fresh eyes.

153. Limits on self-plagiarism. Although plagiarism is a no-no, under some circumstances you can appropriately integrate the published text of one of your old findings in a new publication if it is relevant. But do not base very much of the new manuscript on text you published previously. Some journals set explicit limits on how much of your own previously published text you can include in a new article. Make sure you get something in writing from the publisher on how much previous content you can include. When in doubt, leave it out.

154. Citations. When you write an article, you cite other researchers who preceded you. Once your article is published, other scholars will cite you and so your citation count begins. Sixty years ago, the Institute for Scientific Information developed software to count how many times an article was cited. Today that technology is incorporated in Google Scholar. While there are other, highly respected, citation-counting organizations, Google Scholar has become the standard of reference. You will find that many professors list their Google Scholar citation count (and the associated measures we discuss below) on their webpage.

Your article citation counts are an important part of your academic record, but a limited measure of your productivity. A full assessment of your research productivity, for example, the assessment made by an appointment, promotion, and tenure (APT) committee, should include: reading your publications; evaluating whether and how they have made a significant contribution to the literature; noting whether you have authored some publications by yourself; noting whether you have been the lead author in co-authored publications; differentiating books from articles, etc. However, beware: Some APT committee members may reify and prioritize your citation score above all other indicators. A few actually may look *only* at your citation score. We believe that these behaviors are a dereliction of duty. They cannot begin to capture the contributions you have made. But it is in your interest to pay attention to your citation score.

ON WRITING

Hint 155 A citation is a citation whether it is a positive or negative mention of your work.

155. More on citations.

- Because the software does not filter out self-citations, you can boost your numbers simply by repeatedly citing yourself. We strongly discourage this practice.
- A citation is a citation whether it is a positive or negative mention of your work. We knew a respected scholar who applied a new analytical technique but made a mistake. After that, other researchers cited him, warning, "Be sure not to do what Jones (not their real name) did." Jones, however, wound up with an impressively high citation score.
- While your authorship order can help tell your story, it is not part of the citation count. For example, as first author, you established yourself as the lead of the project. In many domains, last author is a senior level person. Regardless of your position, your citation is counted exactly the same. Wherever you fall in the authorship order, you should try to be before #5 as in many references after #6 you are grouped together with "et al." and your name is never seen.

156. Develop a pool of research references stored in your computer. This is one of the most useful things you can do. You will use the same references over and over as you do research, as you write papers, and as you teach. You will add to this list as you read new articles and books in the literature. Invest early in a bibliography manager. There are many online and a number of them integrate with word processing software and database search software (e.g., PubMed, Google Scholar, etc.). We personally recommend the software EndNote®,[2] although other similar kinds of software are on the market and universities likely provide one for free.[3] Software for references contains three useful features:

- It provides a standard form for entering references so you remember to include all the necessary data. Separate forms are provided for each type of reference (books, articles, newspapers, Internet URLs, etc.).
- It automatically converts the format to the reference style of a particular journal. Lots of different styles are available. Since you may be sending an article to several journals sequentially before it is accepted (see Hint 4), this automated feature saves you hours of drudgery converting reference formats.
- It provides space for including abstracts and notes so you can record what the reference was about for future retrieval.

157. Reuse the literature search from your dissertation. If you conducted a thorough literature search for your dissertation, you will never need to do one again if you write in the same area. If you write in an adjacent field or on an adjacent topic or want to include the latest reference, your cycle time for the literature search is much, much shorter. Remember too that your students or graduate assistants will perform some of the slogging necessary for a literature search.

158. Deadlines. Many graduate students and professors hate deadlines even though they pervade academic life. If your dissertation isn't completed and approved by a specific date, you do not march at graduation. Requests for proposals require submission by a certain date. Book publisher's contracts and professional meetings have deadlines for submitting a polished draft. Grades are due shortly after the end of the semester or trimester. The list goes on.

The truth is that deadlines are friends, not enemies. They force you to finish and free your mind to move on to the next task. We know academics who lament that were it not for a deadline their article or proposal would be much better. We doubt that. We estimate that three additional months spent on an article or proposal improves a manuscript by, at most, 15 percent. It's better to have completed an excellent paper than to never finish the perfect paper. This goes for your dissertation. Finish it.

NOTES

1 R. Allen, ed., *Pocket Fowler's Modern English Usage* (New York, NY: Oxford University Press, 2006); W. Strunk Jr. and E. B. White, *The Elements of Style,* 4th ed. (New York, NY: Longman, 1999).

2 For more information on *End Note,* go to www.endnote.com

3 Popular free online bibliography managers at the time of this writing include: https://www.zotero.org/ and https://www.mendeley.com

Chapter 8
On Publishing

Hint 168 Publish early and often.

At several points along the way, we stressed the need for you to publish if you are going to survive in a research-oriented institution. In this section (and in the subsections on journals and on book publishers), we present what you need to know about the publication process. Also, go back to Hint 4 (Drew's Law), which tells you every good article can find a home.

159. Submit your best articles to the best journals in the field. Work your way down the list if an article is rejected. Many articles rejected by a poor journal were later accepted by a leading journal, so you might as well start with the best. It is easier to follow this rule if you are thick skinned.

Two additional factors should affect where you place a journal on your go-to list (not all journals make this information public): the percentage of submitted articles the journal accepts, and the average length of time it takes for the staff to review a submission.

160. Keep track of your submissions. Submissions get lost. It is up to you to keep track of your submissions relative to the average length of time for a review. We all have horror stories about lost submissions and the multiple rounds of follow up that ensued. One of us recants a recent submission to a very well-respected journal where she wanted her work considered for publication and it had an average time to review of about five months. After numerous follow-up emails, the editor in charge went silent on her. She looked up the editorial board and emailed some of her colleagues for help. She finally got the paper published . . . after 580 days! We suggest that you stay more on top of your submissions than that timeline would suggest, but do not be afraid to reach out to your resources for assistance.

161. Write most of your articles for refereed journals. Papers presented at meetings get you funds to be a world traveler. However, even if refereed, conference papers don't typically count for tenure, promotion, or salary raises. However, sometimes conferences will have a relationship with a journal and offer fast-tracked publication of your conference paper. This is usually indicated in the conference call for papers.

162. Avoid writing introductory textbooks if you are not tenured. You can make a lot of money writing textbooks; however, many of these books wind up taking so much time you would be financially better off if you had worked for minimum wage at a fast food joint. Most tenure committees think of them as moonlighting, not scholarly productivity.

Your colleagues will assume you are doing it for money (called dirty money by some), which allows you to live in a better house and wear better clothes than they do. This attitude is particularly evident in those who took (an implicit) vow of poverty when they joined academe. If you're a senior professor whose book sells, you will be praised for enhancing the department's reputation as well as your own (Hint 3). However, the jealousy will still be there.

163. Recognize the difference between writing the first paper on a subject and writing the nth one. Writing the first paper requires a special knack for originality, which few people have. A first paper usually is not very deep, but it creates enough of an impact that others will follow your lead and write deeper scholarly works. The advantage of the first paper is that it is always referenced, giving you a long list of citations. If you are fortunate enough to have the knack, you will need to market your output carefully. Journals (and reviewers) look for the tried and true. Journals, after all, publish almost exclusively on subjects they've published previously. Members of tenure and promotion committees will read your paper and say it is trivial because they have read the more careful articles others wrote later based on your idea. It has been our observation that people who write first papers possess a different set of skills from those who write the nth ones and should leave the writing of the nth papers to someone else.

164. Writing the nth paper means that $n-1$ papers on the subject were written before yours. Although you need not cite all of them, you should cite enough authors of previous papers for some of them to be selected as reviewers. (One of the secrets of the journal business is that editors find reviewers by looking in the reference lists for names of people they know.) You may, however, be unfortunate enough to have someone you did not cite selected to review your article. If so, the reviewer will probably comment that you failed to include their citation, which, of course, is a dead giveaway of the reviewer's name.[1]

165. When writing the nth paper, make sure your contribution to the issue is clear. Whether your contribution is a carefully conducted experiment or an elaboration of the theory or a synthesis and interpretation of previous work, be explicit in saying it. Reviewers need to be convinced the manuscript contains something new that merits publishing.

166. Revise papers quickly. As an author, you don't help the publication production process if you take a long time between receiving reviews and submitting the revised article.

167. Turn around your reviews of other people's papers quickly. Reviewing is a scarce resource and important work. You want your work reviewed quickly, and you should show the same courtesy to others. Don't be too busy to review, and return the article quickly.

168. Publish early and often. N matters, even though $N + 2$ is required for tenure (see Hint 1). Begin writing for publication while you are still in graduate school. Data show that people who publish while still in graduate school usually continue to publish at a faster rate after they graduate than those who didn't publish while still a student. Furthermore, published papers and monographs help you get your first job.

169. Your dissertation is a publishing asset. You should receive a return on your investment for the time you spent on your dissertation. Avoid advisers who insist on joint authorship with them on all papers that result. They are exploiting you. One paper with your dissertation adviser or committee is satisfactory for a one-paper dissertation, but including a coauthor is not necessary for every paper that follows. For a three-paper dissertation, your chair should be on each of the papers as well as the subject matter experts. In this model, sometimes the subject matter expert only contributes to that one paper.

170. The literature search you performed for your dissertation is a treasure trove of information. It should be the foundation of a survey article on the field. And the world desperately needs more survey articles. You may need to search deep for a journal that will accept this type of paper. Note that a literature review is not the same as a meta-analysis and may not carry as much "weight" on tenure and promotion review. You will be rewarded more for adding one little new data point to the literature than for a brilliant synthesis of that literature (unless your name is Arnold J. Toynbee).[2] You can, however, transform a literature review into a meta-analysis, which is a systematic, statistical aggregation of previously published research findings. Such a paper carries more cachet with tenure committees, and the statistics are not difficult to compute.

171. Include single-author papers in your portfolio. Review committees wonder about people who always publish with someone else and are smooshed in the mix somewhere. Did they do the work or did they ride the coauthor's coattails? Were they the first author? If you must coauthor, pick people whose names follow yours alphabetically and then suggest that your name really belongs first. If you are unfortunate enough to be named Zyzygy, go to court and get it changed.

172. Co-authoring a paper with a superstar. Doing so increases your visibility and associates you with their reputation. However, be careful which papers you coauthor. If the idea is yours, the superstar will likely get most of the credit.

173. Be aware of delays in publishing. You face long, long delays. In this hint we estimate the delays in journal publication; for books, the total time is usually much longer. Let's assume you've written your first article and have the final draft that is ready to send off to the top journal in the field. If you expect that this brilliant piece will appear in the next issue or, at the latest, the one after that, we have a bridge to sell you in Brooklyn. Let's assume your article is so good it is accepted without a request for even minor revisions. Even in this unusual case, the pace of publication is extremely slow. To help you understand the timeline and potential time delays, we've created the diagram below. This figure shows typical workflows. Some publishers are more streamlined than others, but they all have bottlenecks that can substantially increase your time to publication. Note that if you add up all of the average times in the figure, it could take over a year to get your manuscript published. We are very generous in this best-case assessment; in real life, longer periods are not at all unusual, especially for top-tier journals (see Hint 159).

At this point you can claim publication if the article is accepted for publication. If revision is required, you need to add the time you take to revise, the time the reviewers spend agreeing that the revisions meet their standards, and exactly the same delays in writing emails as for the original draft. We leave it, as the mathematicians say, as "an exercise to the reader" to compute the delay if one, two, or three revisions are required. But you're not the proud possessor of your name in print yet.

Many of the numbers in the printing process are quite broad. For example, if a journal is published quarterly, an extra three month's delay may come just from your being the $N + 1$st article for an issue of N articles in a quarterly.

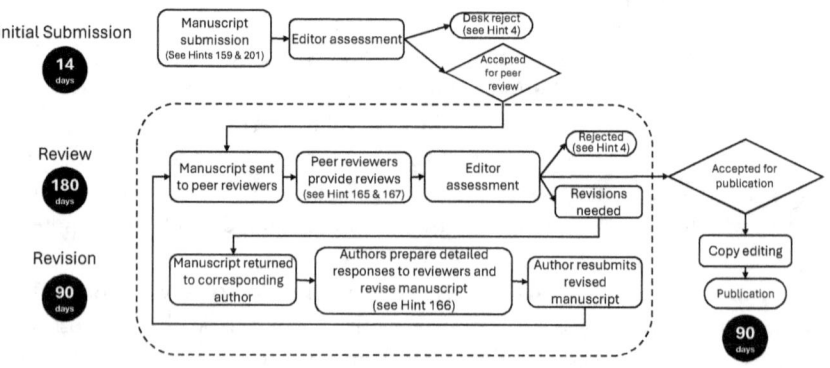

Total publishing time, from initial submission to final publication, can take up to a year and can involve multiple revisions (dotted line indicating a potentially repeatable process) – see Hint 192.
Sometimes, open access journals accelerate the process, but the overall process is the same for open and closed access journals (see Hint 194). Plan accordingly and make sure that you follow up with the editor if any of the reviews are beyond their published time frame (see Hint 160).

174. Rewards for academic publishing. The old saw "Virtue is its own reward" applies to most academic publications. There are exceptions. For a scholarly monograph in the humanities or the social sciences, you may receive a small royalty. Journals invariably do not pay. Your annual review to determine whether you should receive a raise, however, tends to reward you for publishing, particularly in highly reputed journals. Of course, if you work abroad in a school such as one we know about in South Korea, you may be awarded a bonus every time you publish, with the size of the bonus depending on the prestige of the journal.

ON PUBLISHING

JOURNALS

You rely on journals as outlets for your work. Your relationship with a journal can also include your becoming an editor or a reviewer.

175. Don't become an editor too early. That is, don't accept the impressive title editor-in-chief or department editor of any publication early in your career, regardless of how flattered you feel with being tapped for this task—it could be that the journal could not get anyone else. Journal editing takes time. Don't get involved at the editorial level until your career is well launched. At all costs, avoid editing struggling newsletters, special-interest publications, and the like.

176. Do serve as a reviewer for journals, particularly top journals. Treat this job seriously. You will see much junk being submitted and appreciate why some journals reject 80 percent or more of their submissions. You will develop a sense of what is good and what is not, and you will correspond with some powerful people (Hint ?). When you do get a good article to review, you will receive much earlier knowledge of an important new development, which is worth more than the time you take reviewing the article.

BOOK PUBLISHERS

Although the Internet and multimedia are here, the foreseeable future will still include textbooks and monographs. Book publishers are like honeybees bringing intellectual pollen you need for your classes. Publishers are outlets for your books (but see Hint 162 about the trade-off in writing textbooks).

177. Pay attention to the book publishers' representatives who contact you. They are a valuable source of information. These reps have two missions: to flog the books their company issues and to send intelligence back to the home office. They will be pleased to send you complimentary copies of the latest mass market elementary textbooks in your field; although be prepared as many of those may not be physical books, but rather e-books. If your field is French, you can obtain many shelves of freshman- and sophomore-level French books. You can also obtain copies of books directly linked to specific courses you teach. It is a little more difficult (but not impossible) to obtain complimentary copies of books in your research area. There's always the chance that you will adopt one of these for your courses.

Don't, however, simply look at the reps as a source of freebies. Use them to find out what is going on in the book market. Sound them out on whether their company is interested in a book manuscript you have under way. Their response

85

will usually be positive. Ignore that. Just make sure they get the word about your forthcoming manuscript back to the editors at the publisher's headquarters.

178. Selecting a publisher involves trade-offs. With a large publisher that issues many books in your field in a year you gain the advantage of mass marketing and advertising. Large publishers employ reps who visit campuses and send lots of emails. However, these reps are given many books to push, and their commissions depend on the number of books sold. As a result, they concentrate on freshman and sophomore texts for required courses. Furthermore, since they receive the same commission no matter which book they sell, they have little incentive to sell a particular book. Thus, you run the risk that the promotion of your book will be lost among the many others with similar titles being offered by that publisher.

Small and specialty commercial publishers and university presses give you much more individual attention. You can judge whether they are a good fit for your book by looking at their publications list on their websites, the mailings you receive from them, the advertisements in your professional journals, and the experience and recommendations of your peers.

If a publisher looks reasonable based on these probes, go to your school's library and look at its books. Before signing a contract, make sure your publisher will have your manuscript peer reviewed, and the publisher you chose counts with your field's tenure committee. Unless all else fails, do not publish with a vanity press, that is, a company that charges you for publishing your book.

179. Get to know the major editors of the book publishers in your field. The best place to meet them is at the book exhibits at your annual professional conferences. You will find that some of them know absolutely nothing about your field, not to mention your subject. Avoid working with such editors because they will treat your work as a commodity, like pork bellies.

NOTES

1 Some argue you should cite everyone whoever wrote on a subject. This approach is not desirable and often not feasible. If the subject is well published, you can never be certain you found every (obscure) reference, your list of references would be extremely long, and too long a list may be held against you. It's better to take your chances on finding the relevant references and citing those.

2 https://archives.history.ac.uk/makinghistory/historians/toynbee_arnold.html. Accessed January 6, 2024.

Chapter 9
Tenure

Hint 192 Know the tenure clock.

The most dreaded experience for an academic is the tenure process. Without tenure, you cannot stay permanently at an institution as a professor, and you must go job hunting in an uncertain market. Some schools may consider it a stain on your record if you tried but failed to obtain tenure; with it, you remove the uncertainty.

Some large, often unionized, state institutions undertake incremental reviews that reduce the trauma by letting people know where they stand as they go along. Others undertake stringent three-year reviews in which some are fired and others are given warnings and firm instructions on what they should do over the next three years to gain tenure. However, because administrators and criteria can change, these reviews do not guarantee tenure will be granted.

180. Tenure is the prize. Although things are changing and institutions are moving away from offering tenure-track positions, it is still true that tenure is the goal in academia. Many non-tenure-track jobs are exciting in higher education and in research organizations, but most new PhDs seeking academic careers want to become tenured professors.

181. Your promotion dossier. When you are reviewed for tenure or promotion, the review committee relies on a dossier about your work, usually prepared by the committee chair. At most institutions, you prepare the first draft of that dossier. This is an opportunity! Review committees and committee chairs are often lazy. They probably will not edit your text heavily, so if you say, "Professor Jones is the most productive, creative sociologist in the last 50 years," they might leave this sentence in the final draft.

Typical dossiers consist of:

- An introduction, including the review process
- A brief description of your career before appointment, i.e., your education and prior employment
- Your research program, if you are at a research university
- A detailed description of your publications (usually with copies of publications enclosed)
- Your approach to teaching and your teaching reviews
- Comments from student letters solicited for the review, which are signed by the students at some institutions, although their names and identifying text are redacted to protect confidentiality
- Your program, department, school, university, and professional service.

Your review committee chair obtains the outside reviewers, student letters, and describes the review process. You prepare the rest.

Preparing a dossier is an onerous chore. Some items, like teaching evaluations and even copies of your publications, may be difficult to find.

182. Start your tenure dossier on your first day of employment. We recommend you begin setting up a dossier the week you begin the position and accumulate elements for it as they become available. To do this, we strongly suggest that you start a document in which your tenure and promotion guidelines from the faculty handbook are used as headings—these are the metrics by which you will be evaluated for tenure and promotion—and then document, document, document. As you accomplish things in these headings, just put in quick bullet points. This will become the outline for your dossier narrative. It will be much easier to compile your artifacts and your accomplishments incrementally than all at one time at the end. Then, you will not be in the frenzy that your colleagues are in trying to gather everything at the last minute (and then a storm hits and your system dies).

183. Why tenure is such a hurdle. Consider the cost of a positive tenure decision to your institution. Let's assume that you are making $100,000.00 when you come up for tenure and will serve the university 30 years after tenure. Assume your academic raises only cover the cost of living (the worst case from your point of view, the best from the university's); that is, your salary is nearly the same in real terms for the rest of your career. From your point of view, you certainly think of yourself as worth the $3 million bet the university must make. But think of it from the university's viewpoint. If it awards tenure when it shouldn't, the school made a bad $3 million bet. If it denies tenure to someone and that person many years later wins a Nobel Prize, everyone will conclude, "That university sure was stupid." However, that buzz will last only for a few days, and the affair will blow over. Nobody remembers the names of the universities who chose not to hire Albert Einstein. Although it will cost the school something to hire your replacement if you are denied tenure, with any luck your replacement will work for even less than you did. Any statistician will tell you that given these upside and downside risks, universities are absolutely rational to err on the no side, not on the yes side of granting tenure.

184. Once you achieve tenure, never take another appointment without it. The people who promise tenure "real soon" may not be there when the crunch comes. See Hint 1.

185. Tenure, like research support (Hint 184), can be negotiated on the way in. Nobody tells you (and nobody admits it), but tenure is, in effect, transferable. Be firm in your position that you wouldn't think of moving without being tenured at the new institution.

186. Tenure is tougher to obtain in cross-disciplinary fields. You are judged by the standards of people who made their mark in a single, well-established discipline. For example, information systems, which is taught in business schools, combines a hard science (computer science) and two soft sciences (organizational behavior and management). People in this field publish at the intersection of disciplines; however, they are judged by people in the pure disciplines and are expected to contribute to these pure disciplines. Research that combines existing ideas from several disciplines is discounted by purists even though it is the essence of the field.

187. Once you achieve tenure, don't stop working. It's true that after you become a tenured professor, you cannot be fired (except for rare circumstances; see Hint 189). You may experience an understandable temptation to rest on your laurels. You have earned a rare gift, guaranteed lifetime employment. Instead, seize the opportunity to invest more energy in your teaching, mentoring, research, writing, and service, knowing that you have removed the Sword of Damocles that was hanging over your head. Also, you now have the freedom to make sure that your work/life balance is healthy. You may wish to consult one of the many books or coaches that communicate expert advice about balance (also, see Chapter 15).

188. Once you achieve tenure, don't stop learning. Embrace lifelong learning. Even a hard-working, tenured professor may be tempted to teach the exact same material from year to year. Try to stay fresh and on the cutting-edge of your discipline. Keep up with the latest theories, quantitative and qualitative research methods, and research findings. As noted in Hint 233, you may be able to have much of this new information sent to you automatically.

Additionally, theories, models, and methods from another field may have potential value in your field. Sewall Wright developed multiple linear path analysis in the 1920s because of its potential value in his field of genetics. In 1966, sociologist Otis Dudley Duncan published an article about path analysis in the *American Journal of Sociology*. It was a technical article with a number of formulas, but its basic message was, "The geneticists have this technique called path analysis; maybe it would be useful in the social sciences."[1] That article started what became a tsunami of path analysis studies in the social sciences. And path analysis led to structural equation modeling. Duncan won awards for his article. He deserved them; he made a real contribution. And he illustrated how theories and models from one field can have a major positive impact in another.

189. Tenure is forever (almost). When forever ends, you retire. There is a roughly 50 percent chance you will be involved with your tenured colleagues longer than you will be connected to your spouse or partner.

We know of only two exceptions to this professional lifetime commitment, and since both happen rarely, we don't think you should lose sleep over them.

- If the university closes your department, technically it has the right to dismiss the professors in that department. Even then, however, administrators

can choose instead to reassign professors to other departments or help them find another position. Remember too (Hint 184), if you move to another school, tenure is usually transferable.
- You can be fired if the university claims moral turpitude. These offenses can take the form of a felony, theft from the university, plagiarism, and more. If university administrators want to fire you, they look for alleged moral turpitude that would make headlines in the *National Enquirer* to let them off the hook.

190. Tenure as we know it today may not be here forever. The problem stems from changes in the retirement law and in public attitudes. Since 1992, you can no longer be forced to retire once you reach the "mandatory retirement age." Thus, universities that grant tenure are stuck with you as long as you want to work, whether you perform or not. The teaching life is fulfilling, and the paycheck is better than your retirement income (which gets even better when you can take money out of your tax-deferred retirement nest egg and still collect your paycheck as well as your Social Security benefits). Besides, what would you do with yourself in retirement? When our colleague, the late Peter Drucker (who was still teaching at age 92), was asked why he didn't retire, he replied, "Why retire at 65? I can't see myself driving a Winnebago for 25 years."

191. The number of tenured slots may decrease with time. According to the American Association of University Professors (AAUP) and specific to the US,[2] 48 percent (rounded) of the academic workforce is part-time, 24 percent full-time tenured, and 13 percent full-time non-tenure-track. These data, through fall 2021, show full-time tenured and full-time non-tenure-track trending in opposing directions with the former trending downward and the latter trending upward. At the current rate, full-time non-tenure-track could cross over by 2030, meaning that there could be a greater number of full-time non-tenure track than full-time tenure track faculty by 2030. Additionally, full-time tenure-track is on the decline at 9 percent, with 7 percent of faculty at an institution with no tenure. As the non-tenure-track offerings continue to increase, full-time tenured faculty will continue to decrease. It is not clear whether this change is the result of universities hedging their bets because they fear enrollments will go down in some areas, a deliberate move to reduce the size (and with it, the power) of the tenured faculty, or universities simply want to reduce their payroll.

THE MECHANICS OF TENURE

192. Know the tenure clock. Should you be fortunate enough to be on the tenure-track, make sure you understand the tenure clock at your university. You will likely have a review at the mid-point and then usually have an extra year to find a job at the end, should you not be granted tenure. So, let's assume that your university says that you must go up for tenure (submit your dossier) in year six. You will likely have a review at year three (Hint 181) with about 18 months to accomplish the guidance given by the committee that, in their experience, will have you positioned for tenure. If your committee says you are light on publications, keep in mind that you need to write the manuscripts and that those can take a year to actually get published. If you are denied tenure, and you are at the end of your university's tenure clock, they may offer you a contract or give you one year to find a job.

193. The dreaded impact factor. Not only are schools ranked (Hint 77) from lowest to highest, but so are academic journals. The Institute for Scientific Information in Philadelphia created a measure it calls the *impact factor*, a numerical measure of prestige for each journal. For a given journal, it is based on dividing the number of citations that year to articles published in that journal in the previous two years divided by the number of papers published in the journal in those two years. For example, an impact factor of 3 means that, on average, the articles published in that journal in the previous two years have been cited three times.

Although the system may seem unfair and a poor approximation for long-term impact, the numbers produced are considered holy. The ratings are published with fanfare by journals that receive high rankings.

Worse, many tenure and promotion committees use these numbers to judge whether your work is important. Fortunately, not all your publications have to be in top-ranked journals. Tenure committees usually also look for bulk, that is, how many publications you wrote. You are allowed to (and should) find journals to publish your less valuable articles (i.e., stinkers) to obtain bulk (Hints 1 and 4).

194. Open access vs. closed access. What is the difference and what should you look for? The primary difference between open access and closed access journals is the business model. The business model of open access journals is that the author pays an article processing fee and the business model of closed access journals is that there is a subscription fee for readers of the journal (we suggest that you negotiate some article processing fees into your job offer and always include them in grant proposals under dissemination of study). Absent the subscription fee, there is a per article cost. There are other differences to be aware of though. For example, open access journals allow for wider dissemination of your research, because the barriers to access are removed. This can lead to higher citation rates and higher impact factors (Hints 154, 193, and 195).

In open access journals, the author typically retains copyright, but that may not always be the case. In contrast, closed access journals have chosen to restrict access to those who pay a subscription or those with institutional access. In this case, the publisher retains the copyright. Many of the traditional closed access publishers also have an open access option. Both models typically require peer review to ensure rigorous scientific methods have been followed and reported.

However, open access has led to a new category of journal—predatory journals. Predatory journals exploit the open access business model without the assurance of scientific rigor. Predatory journals can be difficult to identify. The first thing to look for is an association with a reputable publisher. Additionally, you want to take note of the publishing standards, the editorial oversight, and indexing. The *Directory of Open Access Journals* (DOAJ.org) is an excellent resource to gather information on open access journals. They also publish a check list called Think Check Submit (https://thinkchecksubmit.org/journals) where answering questions helps to identify predatory journals.

195. Impact factor turned upside down. It stands to reason that the more accessible a journal paper, the more it will be cited. The more that it is cited, the higher the impact factor. Enter open access journals. Impact factors were developed before open access publishing when all journals were subscription-based only—in other words, the author submitted the paper, the paper got accepted, the author signed away copyright, the paper got printed, and other scholars accessed your paper through either a university library subscription or a professional subscription. In 1991, 30 years after impact factor was developed, Paul Ginsparg established open access at Los Alamos National Laboratory to make work developed by the physicists freely available (arXive); however, arXive is not peer-reviewed, it is thought of more as pre-review. These papers still needed to be published in a peer-reviewed journal with an impact factor. However, around 2000, the idea of open access journals became more mainstream and involved authors paying an article processing fee (APF), oftentimes retaining copyright. APFs can cost an author anywhere from $500 to $5,000.

196. Tenure committees look almost exclusively at refereed publications that appear in peer-reviewed journals or in scholarly books. It is, in a sense, a tragedy that you get much more credit for what appears in a *write only* journal (i.e., a journal with a minute circulation) than for what appears in a high circulation, widely read popular magazine. But that is the way the game is played.

197. Downloads count. Members of tenure and review committees like candidates who develop a personal reputation, thus reflecting glory on the institution. Impact factors (Hints 193 and 195) are one crude measure. Another is the download count, which means that if you have an academic publication that is accessible on the Internet, is anybody reading it, or better still, downloading it? Some publishers record download counts and send them to authors. If you are fortunate enough to receive download counts, keep them. They are handy at tenure and performance review time. (See Hint 199 for other publishing metrics.)

198. Multiple-author papers. In Hint 171 we advise you to make sure you are the sole author of some of your publications and tell you of the risks of being a coauthor with superstars. We do not imply that being a coauthor is risky or dangerous. It is not. Working with people you know, even if they are at another institution far away, can be exhilarating because of the spark of ideas as you play off one another. In some fields (e.g., chemistry and medicine) lengthy author lists are the norm, particularly if a project is large. However, many journals are starting to limit the number of authors on a paper.

Early in a research project, you and your coauthors need to discuss candidly the order of the names on the publication. Have this discussion long before the article is about to be submitted; otherwise, it becomes a fight of who did more work and that can turn ugly very quickly.

199. What are key citations indices? Are they important? The i-10 index, specific to Google Scholar, reflects the number of publications with at least 10 citations (e.g. an i10-index of 15, means the author has 15 papers that have been cited at least 10 times each). The h-index (Hirsch index) is a measure of both the productivity and citation impact of the author's work. The h-index is expressed in terms of the researcher's most cited papers and the number of citations they have received. For example, an h-index of 15 means that a researcher has published 15 papers, each of which has been cited at least 15 times. It indicates that the researcher has had significant impact, as demonstrated by a substantial number of citations to their work. The g-Index is preferred by some, but is not routinely reported by Google Scholar. It is the largest number of papers you have published, which when squared, is equal to or less than your total number of citations. For example, if you have published 22 papers and your total number of citations is 400, your g-Index is 20 (since 20 squared equals 400). Consider two scholars. Dr. Smith has published one article which has received 900 citations. Dr. Jones has published 30 articles which collectively have received 900 citations. The g-Index for Dr. Smith is 1. The g-Index for Dr. Jones is 30.

200. Boosting your index. Regardless of the index, g, h, or i . . . or future indices that come out . . . there are ways to boost your citations, and thus, your index. However, in doing so, it is critical to remember that this can take a long time—sometimes as long as a decade. Don't be afraid to self-promote, but be very careful not to self-cite excessively. Publish in highly cited journals for your field. Collaborating with others connects you to their networks and can also lead to increased citations. Ensure that your abstract is descriptive of your paper. Many people search by, and make decisions from, only the abstract. Ensure common key words and phrases are used in the abstract. You can have the best paper, but if someone needs to read it to decide whether they want to cite it or not, you may lose that citation because the abstract did not provide enough motivation for them to read it in the first place. Well-written systematic literature reviews are often heavily cited. Learn how to do one and then publish.

Google Scholar will notify you when someone cites your work. Reach out to other authors who cite your work, or at the very least, read what they wrote and cited. Contribute to discussion boards—either through social media (see Hint 256 on your digital visibility) or on professional association discussion boards—and alert others when you have published something relevant, or post a digital abstract of your work (Hint 194).

201. Publication quality counts. While we think academic priorities should be different, in real life, tenure committees focus almost exclusively on publications in peer-reviewed journals, the higher they are ranked and the more impact (Hints 193 and 195) they have, the better. Of course, the quantity of your publications is also critical (Hint 1).

Value quality highly. Try to make each article you submit to a journal about a single topic of importance. Conduct your research with a solid, rigorous design. Write as clearly as possible. The paper does not need to be complex—it needs to be understood. *Try to produce each article as though it were the one example of your work that will be remembered.*

202. Rolling reviews. University administrators' objective is different from yours. They want to avoid deadwood, and they take age as *prima facie* evidence of your being too old. They certainly want you out of there before the effects of old age impede your performance. If the number of positions is constricted, the administration would prefer to take your slot and give it to a bright young person who is more current, may work for less, and who revitalizes your department. Tenure forces a university to hold on to you because firing you because of your age would be discrimination. Younger faculty who want new opportunities generally side with the university. As a result, some universities have introduced a *rolling* tenure arrangement in which tenured full (and sometimes associate) professors are reviewed every five years and may be encouraged to leave because of poor performance.

The mechanics of the eternal five-year rolling review, while usually not as rigorous as tenure itself, look at what you've accomplished. Such tangibles as teaching evaluations and research publication records are examined by a special faculty committee, often constituted uniquely for each professor. Penalties for poor performance can range from recommendations for improvement in the next five-year interval to a recommendation that you be fired. The latter option is extremely rare, but not unheard of. Most institutions allow several opportunities for improvement. Don't assume tenure protects you against negative five-year reviews.

Our indications are that rolling reviews result in making senior people work a little harder. They became professors because they are risk averse and therefore want to avoid consequences. The best protection against a negative review is to produce as a teacher, a scholar, and as a citizen of your institution (teaching, research, and service).

We recommend you keep your CV up to date and maintain records of what you accomplished from the day you start at your institution. It will make your reviews easier. Furthermore, if the verdict is negative, you have generated the material needed to obtain your next appointment.

NOTES

1 O. D. Duncan (1966) "Path analysis: Sociological examples." *American Journal of Sociology* 72(1): 1–6.

2 https://www.aaup.org/sites/default/files/AAUP%20Data%20Snapshot.pdf

Chapter 10
Academic Rank

Hint 204 As a full professor, you must be known for something.

Just like grade inflation, rank inflation is a sign of our times. It used to be that people with new PhDs were hired as instructors and then rose to assistant, associate, and full professor. Today, only the last three of these remain. Tenure usually is the transition to associate. Full professor is, of course, the desired state. That being said, we have heard of plenty of examples of associate professors without tenure. This happens when they are hired in at the rank of associate professor, but not hired in with tenure.

203. Being a tenured full professor is as close to freedom as you can come in US society. Yes, you must meet your classes. However, when you walk into your office in the morning, it is you who decides what you should be working on, not someone else. You can decide to continue what you have been working on or delve into something new. You are limited only by your imagination. It is a state much desired by others and one you achieved.

204. As a full professor, you must be known for something and, in some institutions, that reach must be international. When you reach the exalted state of tenured associate professor, the time has come to see the big picture and undertake large, long-term research projects so you can become a full professor. Unfortunately, you spent the previous six years (and your dissertation time) doing small, short-term research projects, each designed to earn you a publication or two so you could achieve tenure. You were never taught how to conduct a large project, and therefore you are back into a learning situation. Merely doing more of what you did as an assistant professor doesn't cut it in major institutions because the promotion committees ask different questions. Having survived the tenure process, everyone knows you can do research. But to be a full professor, you must be known for something. If your institution requires an international aspect to your reach, collaborate with researchers from other countries. With video conferencing, this has become easy to achieve, once you identify a collaborator. We suggest that you submit a paper to an international conference and then, while at the conference, seek out people who do similar research. Exchange contact information and then follow up. If you need the international reach, it is up to you to initiate the contact and the project.

205. Avoid becoming the pitied Permanent Associate Professor. It is a dead end. You get all the committee assignments no one else wants. Although people are nice to Permanent Associate Professors, behind their back they cluck about "poor Smith." It is important for you to remember that if you stay an associate professor for too long, the time for promotion passes you by. This interval varies from institution to institution. However, while still an assistant, it will pay you to determine how long it takes people in your school or department to be promoted. Try to be in the middle or get promoted earlier. Remember too that you must have done something to merit promotion.

206. Promotion is a unique opportunity for a larger pay raise. When you are promoted to associate professor, or from associate to full professor, you have the opportunity to request a substantial pay increase. As implied in Hint 53, most universities provide minimal raises for faculty each year; however, many make exceptions for a promotion.

Chapter 11

Your Financial Life as an Academic

Hint 214 Administrators make more to cope with the stress that comes from the many nasty things they need to do.

You should negotiate for the highest initial salary possible, because as we indicated in Hint 53, except for promotion or tenure, you are tied to the average annual raise the institution gives, if any. This chapter discusses some of the factors you need to understand as well as the ins and outs of working now on funding your retirement nest egg.

207. Academics are risk averse. We grant that exceptions exist, but most people going into university teaching are risk averse. They seek security. To them, a dollar at age 70 is as important (or nearly so) as a dollar at age 30. They are willing to take a lower-paying job at 30, because, with tenure, they can expect not to be thrown out on the street at age 50, as happens in the general employment sector, with no possibility of finding another job when a reduction in head count takes place. See Hint 191 on non-tenure positions. Without the guarantee of tenure, you may want to try to negotiate for a higher salary going in.

208. Contracts are given to faculty for nine, ten, or twelve months.[1] It is essential that you understand what your contract terms are. If you are on a nine- or ten-month contract, you are paid your salary for nine or ten months, respectively and the other remaining months are supposedly for you to do with as you please. Usually, professors are paid for an academic year of nine months. For example, if you receive, say, $54,000 a year, you are being paid $6,000 or $5,400 a month, respectively while working. However, the institution usually pays you in 12 installments ($4,500 a month).

If you are on a 12-month contract, you do not have months (typically summer) in your year to do as you please and your salary is over 12 months. Faculty who serve as administrators and some faculty with research grants are paid for 12 months. There are advantages and disadvantages to each type of contract, so make sure that you understand them. For example, in some universities, you can earn up to 50 percent of your salary in the summer instead of just the two or three months of salary, so if you have grants you can make more than your regular salary.

209. Salaries vary by field and by region. Philosophers make less than business school professors, who make less than law school faculty, all of whom make less than physicians teaching in medical schools. For some reason, people in mathematics do well. There are always exceptions in some institutions.

210. Summer pay. The three months "vacation" you receive can, in theory, be spent by you in any way you please. Go to the seashore or abroad, write a book, or work on papers needed for tenure. In practice, young faculty work during the summer for money to supplement the low salaries they accepted. Teaching summer school, if offered to you, is usually paid miserably. See Hint 208 for more on contract lengths.

211. The zero-raise years. Faculty members generally receive a raise in their contract letter for the following year. If you talk with the faculty at conferences or in your own school, they may recall one or more years in which the amount of the raise was zero for everyone, usually because the institutions or legislatures encountered financial difficulty. Because the following year's raise tends to be a percentage of the current year's salary, a zero raise is rarely recovered in future years.

212. Retirement savings. For graduate students and newly minted PhDs, retirement seems like an irrelevant, distant abstraction. It shouldn't be. You should plan for your retirement when you take your first full-time academic job. In Hint 86 we advised you to inquire about the retirement plan before you accept an appointment and told you about the two major faculty retirement systems (the Teachers Insurance and Annuity Association [TIAA] and state plans) in the United States. In this hint, we offer more information about your retirement options.[1]

Of course, some faculty members choose not to retire. As we noted above, our late colleague Peter Drucker was a prime example. Well into his 90s, he continued to teach, consult, and write major books. He never retired from professional activities or the university. He was an exception.

Most professors (including you) do or will retire at some age. Years ago, that age was a mandatory 65. Today, typical professors teach at least until they are 70. At whatever age you retire, you need to consider your retirement finances.

The absolute base is your Social Security income. You and your employer contribute to Social Security as long as you are employed, unless you work in an exempt state system. Unfortunately, your Social Security income will be well below the final salary that you earn.

Most retirement plans involve payroll deductions made by you and contributions by the institution. University plans fall under Section 403(b) of the tax code rather than 401(k) used by industry. There are also 457(b) plans. The plans are different for state and private institutions. Some institutions provide you with a choice among multiple plans but most don't. Retirement money is usually tax sheltered. That is, you don't pay tax on any contribution or its growth until you draw it out after retirement. Especially if you are at a state institution, make sure that you understand how your contributions will work. Many state institutions make you choose between the state plan (your pension) or 403(b) or 457(b) and some will let you invest in all of the plans. This last option, in our opinion, is the home run for building your retirement wealth.

Diversify your investments. Don't put all your money into high-growth stocks that pay off big when the stock market goes up but collapse in an instant if the market tanks, as it did in Fall 2008. In the same vein, don't put all your funds in slow-growth, but safe, blue chip investments, bonds, or bank savings accounts. While they are safer and hedge against dips in the market, you miss the growth and profits in a rising bull market. Many universities offer free investment counseling conducted by the fund—take advantage of it.

Retirement is a consideration when you start your first appointment and when you change retirement plans. If you go from one TIAA institution to another, the plans are almost identical, although the amount of the contributions by the institutions may differ. Going from TIAA to a state system means a different set of rules. The amount you receive from a state system may depend on the number of years of service and the three highest-earning years. Knowing whether you can roll over your account from your present plan to the new one, and how to do that without tax implications, becomes an important factor in evaluating the real income you receive.

Money invested in retirement at a young age yields much more than the same amount invested 20 years later. *Study the compound interest curve.* Essentially the value of your retirement nest egg grows slowly initially. However, because both what you put in and the interest on it is not taxed, your principal eventually skyrockets.

Understand the different fund options. Annuities, for example, were very popular in the 1970s, fell out of favor, and came back (reimagined) in the early 2010s. Annuities are based on the number of years of life expectancy from the date of retirement. Assume you're expected to live until 90 (insurance companies have actuaries who have charts on this stuff). Annuities pay a certain amount monthly, depending mainly on your age and how much you have saved, and these amounts are typically guaranteed for life. Put simply, retiring at 65 leaves you with a smaller nest egg that must be spread over a longer period of time—your remaining life expectancy of 25 years, rather than a larger nest egg if you retire at 75 that will be spread over a shorter period of time—your remaining life expectancy of 15 years.

You can beat this system if you take an annuity and then outlive the actuarial predictions. However, typically funds that have been annuitized are not available to your heirs in your estate. So, if you pass away six months after retiring on an annuity, you will have outsmarted yourself and deprived your heirs of those funds.

Don't retire too early. The longer you stay employed and supported by your regular pay, the more your retirement nest egg grows and the greater the available cash.

Note: Congress is always tinkering with our retirement, including Social Security. It is essential that you stay abreast of these changes.

If you are wise and save now, you will thank us for this advice 40 years from now.

213. Tax deferral. If you can afford it (and unfortunately many young professors cannot) or you receive extra funds such as from consulting or inheritances, put some of the money away as savings for retirement. Various retirement accounts, such as Individual Retirement Accounts (IRAs), simplified employee pension plans (SEPs), and supplemental retirement annuities (SRAs), are available on a tax-deferred basis.[2] If possible, contribute each month to such a plan. The benefits accrued years from now are enormous.

The key point is that your savings are tax deferred, meaning you don't pay taxes now on the amount you save. For example, if you put away $300 per month it only costs you $200 per month. That is, if you didn't invest that $300, you would only see $200 more in your take-home pay.[3] Furthermore, the interest accumulates and your money increases even further. Of course, you eventually must pay the taxes when you use the money, but usually it is at a reduced tax rate if your retirement income is lower than your present income.

Putting away tax-deferred savings, regardless of the vehicle, will also decrease your taxable income at the end of the year. So, if you made $100,000 and stashed away the maximum in your 403(b) account ($23,000 as of this writing, and $30,500 if you are over age 50), the amount that you pay taxes on at the end of the year is $77,000 or $69,500, respectively. This money is much better in your pocket than in Uncle Sam's pocket.

214. Administrators make more. Administrators usually are paid more than professors. Admittedly, most administrators were once professors who abandoned that calling, claiming they should be paid extra to cope with the stress that comes from the many nasty things they need to do. Because they work for the entire year, their pay is based on 12 months. A $54,000 academic salary becomes $72,000 even before a bonus for administration. They may not be off when students are off, but they do get vacation time.

Administrators may not stay administrators forever. For example, if the president or provost changes, the dean may decide that they no longer want to be in that chain of command. In this case, they will likely leave or step back into a faculty position.

NOTES

1 In many schools, particularly private ones, retirement packages for senior faculty are often negotiated privately. Check with recent retirees to find out if such negotiations are available at your school.

2 An alphabet soup of tax deferred plans are available through TIAA, your local bank, and mutual funds. Educational funds provide savings for your children's college tuition. The names and the terms of plans available change over time depending on congressional legislation.

3 The numbers shown assume your federal and state taxes equal roughly one third of your income.

Chapter 12
Life as an Academic

Hint 267 Never, never become a department chair, even an acting department chair, unless you are a tenured full professor.

Now that you know about finding a job, the things you need to do to reach full professor, and the financial aspects of academia, we turn to the things that affect your day-to-day life. This chapter, and sections within it, such as being an institutional citizen, becoming a department chair, and dealing with grievances, should help you understand the life you are preparing to undertake.

215. On becoming a dean. At some point you may be asked to become a dean. In most university hierarchies, dean is the highest administrative position you can hold where you still maintain daily contact with the content and issues in your home discipline. The next step up is provost, or chief academic officer, a position where you lead, manage, and work with the full range of disciplines. (Note that universities vary somewhat in their organizational structures. Some of what we have written about department chairs would apply in some institutions to the dean, and vice versa. We have tried to describe the usual structure.)

You will want to provide leadership that raises your school to a new level. Be aware that professors and universities both change slowly. One of the authors, when he was a dean, used to groan in frustration when trying to persuade faculty members to implement a change that *they* proposed, fought for, and voted for. "I'm convinced that it takes the average professor three hours to watch '60 Minutes.'"

216. Be prepared to spend time on seemingly petty issues. Your faculty colleagues may write articles and books about complex theories, offer hypotheses about deep problems, and conduct sophisticated research, but when you meet with them as dean, they often will be upset about relatively minor, petty issues. Don't be surprised if the issue that generates the most emotion, especially anger, is office space.

217. Sometimes major administrative decisions are made in informal quick conversations. On occasion, you may be asked to agree to a proposal while walking down the hall or across campus. If possible, ask for more time to review the issue and prepare your response. Also, try to anticipate such requests and thoroughly familiarize yourself with the potential issues your school and the larger university will be facing. In short, beware of the 15-second hallway conversation that finds its way into the policy manual because you politely nodded your head.

218. Publishing while "deaning." Your goal may be to provide leadership and initiate major positive organizational changes as dean, while maintaining an active research program. It won't happen. When you step down as dean, you will realize that your research and scholarly activities were minimal during your tenure as dean. One of the authors was a dean for ten years. He always had organized the publication section of his CV by year. He suddenly realized that there was going to be an obvious, embarrassing time gap in which few publications appeared. He then reorganized the publication section by substantive topic.

219. Good deans/Bad deans. Good deans try to make your life better. They help your school and department (and you) increase its reputation. They help in obtaining resources, grants, and chaired positions. Bad deans can make your life miserable. Don't assume that you can outlast them. Two years of a bad dean during the years that you are going up for tenure or promotion could prove very problematic. Keep your CV current.

220. Never, ever choose sides in department politics. The side you are on expects your support because its members know they are right, and they will give you no reward for it. The sides you are not on will remember that forever.

221. Don't accept a joint appointment, particularly as your initial appointment. The chairperson of each department will assume the other chairperson will take care of you. Each department chair will assume they own at least three fourths of you. Furthermore, at raise, promotion, and tenure times, you will be judged by each department only on the papers you published in its own discipline.

222. Join the faculty club if your school has one. You will usually be taken there at some time during the interview process. If it is at all typical, it will seem like a cross between your undergraduate dining hall and the stuffy clubs you see on BBC mysteries. If you look around, it may look like a haven for the superannuated.

Don't be deceived. The faculty club can be one of your most important tools. It is a place where you can meet with colleagues without interruptions by cellphones or students. People always feel better when they eat and will often tell you things they would not otherwise reveal. In other words, it is a good place to keep up with what is going on. Being seen there by the older faculty in your department can be a plus because it shows you want to fit in. You will be surprised to find you can actually have occasional intellectual discussions with people from other disciplines. It is also a good place to impress visitors and students. The food, of course, will rapidly become tedious.

223. Office hours. Although this is somewhat variable with online programs (see next hint), office hours are sacred at some institutions where you *must* be in your office at the times you promise. In other schools, they are merely advisory. Know what the situation is at your institution and follow the local custom. In general, you are required to provide certain times for students when they can contact you. Making appointments is one way to do this. If you do make an appointment, be sure to keep it. A reputation for not keeping appointments is as bad as a reputation for not replying to emails.

224. Online programs. With online programs, students will rely on email, text, and phone as a means of contact, and they may be uncharacteristically informal.

Because of potential time zone differences, traditional office hours (see previous hint) may become a thing of the past. Unfortunately, students expect their communication to be answered as soon as it is sent. We strongly suggest that you make communication responses very clear in your syllabus. For example, you can say that you will answer emails within 72 hours, not including weekends and school holidays/breaks. This requires some flexibility by you also. If your student is in a time zone 12 hours earlier than you, you may need to meet with them at 9 pm your time. This same expectation will likely not exist in face-to-face teaching.

225. Sabbaticals. Although never a guarantee, the best fringe benefit a professor receives is the sabbatical. It is not, repeat not, a vacation. One of us, is writing this book while on her sabbatical. Here are some things you should do on your sabbatical:

- Do productive work.
- Use the time for reflection and getting into new things.
- If at all feasible, leave town and never show your face at the institution during the sabbatical. If you appear, you will be put to work.
- Stay in touch with your dissertation students (by email or by meeting them off campus).
- When your sabbatical is over, write a good report on what you did so the administration will give you another one the next time you are eligible.

As soon as you submit your tenure and promotion packet, read the faculty handbook for information about sabbaticals and always apply for a sabbatical as soon as you are eligible. You may need to apply a year in advance of when you want to take your sabbatical and there may be other constraints imposed by your institution. Make sure that you understand any of the other constraints that apply to sabbaticals—sometimes you may need to advocate for yourself. Most institutions do not allow you to accumulate the time for future use. If you wait an extra semester or two, you may never get the accumulated time back.

226. Maintain collegiality. Collegiality is a difficult term to define. It involves maintaining good social relations with the people in your department and in related departments around campus. If everyone in your department has coffee in the lounge at 10:00 each morning, be there if you can, even if you only drink water. If colleagues ask you to cover a class or review a draft of their latest paper or serve on a doctoral committee they chair, do it. The web of obligations is two-sided and you will receive reciprocal favors over time. Collegiality is one case where the commitments, even though they take away from your research time, yield positive results. Don't be perceived as a loner or a misanthrope, particularly by senior faculty.

227. As an academic you are a public person. Your students spend 40 hours or more a semester doing nothing but looking at or listening to you while you talk. This experience makes an indelible impression on them. You will find several years later when they approach you and call you by name, they will expect you to remember them. You, of course, often will not. Their appearance and dress will be different, and they are not sitting in their usual spot in the classroom. Never say, "Nice to meet you." The alternative is "Nice to see you," which works in all situations. The important point is that your behavior in public places is noticed when you least expect it.

228. On recognizing online students. Online teaching gives you the illusion that you know each student. But you are only seeing a "yearbook photo," or headshot, version of them. Even if you see them a week later on campus, you may not recognize them. Another person's living image or persona includes how they stand and move as well as physical features you have not seen before. The major unknown characteristic is height. While teaching online, you have no idea if a student is 5 feet tall or 6 feet, 6 inches tall.

229. Freedom of speech. We firmly believe that people should be free to express their views on public issues, whether the views are mainstream or not. But understand the associated career risks. The conventional wisdom dictating that academics are free to say what they please may well be the reason why you chose your career. However, our observation of what really goes on leads us to a different take for untenured faculty. No matter what your position on an issue—popular or unpopular, for or against the environment, for or against gun control—once it becomes known, people on the other side of that issue will inevitably surface. They will consider your position a form of bad judgment and they will hold it against you. Remember that people in academia have long memories. Even if everyone in the department publicly espouses the same cause, you cannot be certain what position each one takes privately. Consider something as seemingly safe as excoriating the oil company whose tanker caused the latest oil spill. Your colleagues could be the people who consult with that company, who are writing its corporate history, who have a nephew who works for the company, or who own 3,000 shares of the company's stock. Of course, once you achieve the rank of tenured full professor, the situation changes.

230. Freedom of speech—online. This is markedly different from what you say to colleagues during lunch. What you say on your personal social media accounts matters! We strongly suggest that you keep the lines between you the person and you the academic very far from one another. For example, if your screen name is Best Professor at Your State University and you post something controversial about our government, you could get in trouble—tenure or no tenure. Best to keep your occupation and where you are employed out of your screen name.

231. Attend invited lectures. When world-class people are invited to lecture at your school, regardless of whether or not they are in your field, be sure to attend if at all possible (and definitely if they are among the 100 powerful people in your field as discussed in Hint 2). When you were in graduate school, intellectually important people would come to campus to give seminars and spend a day or two with faculty and students. Often, these were memorable events in your life. You would attend just to see who these people were. Now that you are a faculty member, don't feel too busy to attend such sessions. Even if the topic doesn't seem interesting to you, go. What you will hear, if you listen carefully, is how they think about the world, how they approach problems, and how they work on them. Often, they will change your perspectives in your own areas of teaching and research.

If you are at a small school, you can help bring people to campus to lecture. For example, many professional societies maintain visiting lecturer programs in which people volunteer to visit campuses. Look at the lists and arrange for your department to invite some of them. If you live in a metropolitan area that includes other institutions, get on their mailing list and find out who is coming to visit there. Advertised lectures are open to the public. If you belong to a local chapter of your professional society, work with the program committee to bring interesting people to its meetings.

Remember, lectures are a way to keep up with your field at almost no cost.

232. Serving as an external reviewer. As you advance in your career, someone at another college or university will ask you to write an external review for a person up for tenure or promotion. The first time you receive one of these requests you will probably be flattered and think it a high honor that you are considered sufficiently knowledgeable or important to undertake the task. Unfortunately, it is not an honor, but rather a ritual schools go through because faculty don't believe what they see in front of their eyes. They've lived with the candidate for five or more years. Yet for tenure and promotions, they ask for evaluations from people who at best met the candidate briefly once at a national meeting.

Why do they do it? It is basically an exercise in validation on the candidate's worthiness for tenure or promotion. On one level, they are celebrity hunters, little different from paparazzi. The more well known the evaluator, the better. On another level, they do it because that is the way it was always done, and it might, just might, tell them something damaging they did not know before. Better to be safe than sorry.

Some schools allow the candidate to supply a list of people who should be consulted, some (but not all) of whom will be chosen. That's supposed to make it fairer. The wise candidate includes only personal friends in such a list (there are some limitations, such as you cannot have published with the person). Such evaluations are window dressing because they only yield letters of praise and contain no real information.

The key question often asked of the evaluator—Would you grant tenure to (or promote) this individual at your institution?—dodges the issue, because what is important at your institution is not what is important at the requesting institution. Make sure you read the directions from the chair on what they are looking for in your letter.

Evaluations are considered a free good. Deans and committee members don't value the work that goes into the recommendation because they don't pay for it. Yet hundreds of dollars are spent by your school for your own time and that of the staff involved for each of these evaluations that you write for others. The requesting institution often doesn't even write a thank-you letter, much less let you know the outcome. Your own institution gives you no credit for such work because it is for somebody else. However, if your institution requires evaluations, especially post-tenure, use your request for letters as a measure of your value and regard in the field.

Unless the request is completely outside your field, you shouldn't really avoid the task. Usually, it includes reviewing attached articles and books (you may not be interested in) and writing an evaluation that answers a set of questions. Fortunately, the amount to be written is not extreme. Our experience is that letters of under one page and much over two pages are considered negatively (you're hiding something significant by saying too little or too much). You should be careful even in a two-page letter—make sure that you lay out the letter so that it is easy for the evaluator to follow. If you think the candidate deserves promotion or tenure, be sure not to write an account that discusses positives and negatives. A hint of something negative can be seized upon by a committee member or administrator who is opposed as a reason for saying no. Evaluation letters don't change the underlying politics of the situation.

233. Keeping up with your field. In every field, things change. You can't keep teaching the same material year in and year out. As a faculty member you are committed to lifelong learning. Your need for new knowledge doesn't end with your PhD. You need to keep up with the latest developments in your discipline: new theories, models, research findings, and analytic techniques. Here are some strategies:

- Attend conferences where new ideas are first presented.
- Read the cutting-edge journals and books.
- Use software options, for example, RSS feeds and Google alerts, to keep abreast of new discoveries.

- If you have a research assistant, ask them to find and organize new knowledge for you.
- Make new knowledge the subject for term papers in graduate seminars you teach.

234. Board of trustees. You can work an entire career without ever meeting a trustee or thinking about the board, which is unfortunate because boards of trustees not only wield enormous power over their institutions, they can help individual departments and faculty members like you.

If you work at a state university, the board most likely was appointed by the governor. In private institutions, board policies, including the appointment of new trustees, parallel those of other nonprofit organizations. The president of the institution, or a current board member, proposes a new board member, that person is interviewed, and the full board votes to invite them to join.

Boards of trustees, for example, provide the ultimate vote on whether you receive tenure (almost always pro forma if recommended by the faculty and the administration), provide the monetary pool available for pay increases (typically a percentage of current expenditures), and decide whether and how the university is reorganized.

In most institutions, the board tends to be more politically conservative than the faculty. After all, one of the board members' major functions is to donate money to the institution, and they tend to be wealthy, successful people.

In many institutions, faculty are offered opportunities to meet and talk with board members, such as during receptions, dinners, and retreats. Some boards even have a faculty and a student member. Other boards have the unfortunate tradition of keeping the two groups separate. If you are invited to a board event, attend. Try to get to know one or two board members. They can help you, and they may be able to bring visibility to your research or teaching innovations. In fact, they sometimes introduce you to people and organizations that can fund your work.

YOUR ADMINISTRATIVE LIFE

Even though you are a lone professor, you have an administrative life because you supervise many people, even though they don't work for you, and because you have to interact with administrative people.

235. Secretaries/Administrative assistants are a valuable and scarce resource, and you should treat them as such. Most universities pay secretaries below market wages and expect them to gain psychic income from the academic environment. They often work in physical spaces you would not accept even as a graduate student. (We estimate that the chance of a secretary working in an office with a window is about one in three.) By any standard, they are an exploited class. If you develop a good relationship with them, they will work miracles for you. They know every arcane administrative procedure needed to get things done. They can say nice things about you to people who matter in the department. Remember, however, that if they don't like you, they can kill your reputation.

236. Value your teaching assistants and graders. After years of being one, you know that research assistants and graders are perceived as the sherpas of academe. Their role is to be as inconspicuous as possible and carry the burdens as their professors climb the mountain of knowledge. It is unfortunately true that many young professors rapidly adopt the same attitude. Doing so is a mistake.

237. Grading. Your students learn from the feedback they receive, and graded papers are an important feedback tool. Thus, you need to pay attention to which answers are considered correct and what criteria are used for grading. In the case of examinations, you should grade papers personally rather than delegating the job to a teaching assistant, if you are assigned one. The examination is a form of communication, of feedback, between the student and you. You find out what the students really know and what principles and concepts did not get through to them.

238. Your research assistants require supervision. Having them take data for your key experiment or survey instrument is appropriate, but the final responsibility for their output is yours. You need to know what they are doing and how well they are doing it. Treat them with respect and show them they are valued. One way to do this is to be generous in sharing authorship with them when they make contributions to your research. In short, you must teach them the research art. Remember that disgruntled graders or research assistants need not get mad at you; they can easily get even.

239. Physical plant/Facilities. Like the computer center and other service operations, you must deal with the physical plant or facilities department. The people in physical plant are the ones who provide the services you take for granted: moving furniture or fixing heating or changing light bulbs. Your first contact will typically come when you move into your office.

Many people in physical plant are highly skilled craftspeople who can do wondrous mechanical and electrical things. They know about things you never learned. Physical plant staff work on many jobs simultaneously, and although your job is the one you think is the most important, it is only one of many, some of which are emergencies. Physical plant charges for its services, and often it needs to charge quite a lot because the job is much more complex than you realize. Be sure you have a big departmental budget available before you call physical plant.

240. Be careful what you delegate. As a professor you often delegate work to others, either teaching assistants, department secretaries, or work/study students. Be careful about what you assign and be clear in your instructions. Think of yourself as a supervisor or manager in these situations, which you really are. You will be held responsible for the outcome if they make a mistake. Check their output to make certain it is right. If an error occurs, you will be associated with it, and it will be remembered at the wrong time. Keep in mind that at times the student's or teaching assistant's course work may be of higher priority to them than your assignment, particularly during exam times. You will also find that not all assistants are alike; some need everything defined in detail, others can be given more flexibility.

241. Business cards. When you start out, you want people to remember you and to contact you. It is part of building your image, receiving invitations to participate, and eventually becoming one of the 100 powerful people (Hint 2). Business cards help you achieve these goals. Some departments provide them even to graduate students, particularly if you teach as part of your financial support. If not, they are an inexpensive, and potentially valuable, investment, sometimes as little as $10 or $15. Also, most email systems allow you to create a signature block that appears with every message you send.

Business cards should contain your name, affiliation, and how to reach you via email, Twitter, snail mail, etc. Always carry cards with you. You will use them when job hunting, at conferences, when contacting people about fieldwork, dealing with publishers' representatives, and with students.

YOUR DIGITAL LIFE

242. Keeping all things digital in good working order. You will not be able to function without your digital tools. A laptop for computing, a cell phone for communicating and texting, and a tablet for electronic notes. Although some of your older colleagues still resist multiple digital tools and their various uses, you will be immersed in all things digital. You will know much of the information you find in this section; however, we believe some of it will be new and useful.

243. Learn the idiosyncrasies of your institution's computer center/ IT shop.[1] These are the group of people you will call when your university owned computer system is behaving badly. Regardless of your own ability, the probability of your having to deal with IT is extremely high. Although IT is a service organization, it is sometimes staffed by people who are not service oriented. This attitude is particularly true of directors. Treasure the director who is service oriented. If your center's director is not service oriented, your frustration level will be high every time you need to contact them for help with your computer. Some directors and IT platforms are super security conscious, sometimes making it near impossible to search for what you need to do your research or build your course content. For example, if your research is on illicit drug use in underage populations, you may find many of the websites blocked when you try to visit them.

244. Electronic mail (email). For better or for worse, this is how much of your communication across campus and in your own department will occur. The benefits are several:

- It is efficient—send it when you want, read it when you want, respond when you want.
- It is expeditious—the time between a thought in your head and that thought getting transmitted to the recipient is but a moment.
- No geographic boundaries—you can send email to the next office or right across the world.
- There will always be a record of the communication—don't ever discard any email as this serves as a record and as tracking of the communication.

There are also some drawbacks to email:

- Email lacks emotion—even if you use emojis, it is very easy to misunderstand the tone of email.
- Velocity and volume—unless you turn your email off during the day, you can be under a near constant barrage of emails, very few of which truly need to be answered immediately.
- Forwardability—just assume that whatever you write in an email will be forwarded.
- Public—even if you encrypt your email, if you are sending it from a university owned email account, assume that it is being read by someone other than the intended recipient. It is possible that the unintended recipient is a newspaper reporter. Never send an email that you could not tolerate seeing on the front page of your local newspaper.

If an email goes back and forth three times, pick up the phone and call the person or walk to the person's office. If you find yourself getting anxious or frustrated, pause before sending the email. As we said, rarely will there be an emergency email. And lastly, remain professional. Remember, someone other than the intended recipient is likely going to read that email. We have had numerous situations where we were forwarded an email and we know that the original writer only intended us to see the last communication and not the entire string.

245. Phishing. Email is often used for phishing. Phishing is the malicious attempt to induce the email recipient to give up their credentials (i.e. user name and password). There are various types of phishing that are very targeted, for example at CEOs, or where the sender seems to have some of your information already. Recently, phishing has expanded to text messages (called smishing and vishing) where you get a text message (frequently from a financial institution) alerting you of potential fraud and giving you a link to click. Because you are vigilant, you click the link and it goes to a website that captures your bank information. You see the irony of this? Email is also used in an attempt to load malware and spyware on to your computer when you open a file. You never want to be the one that the IT folks talk about as having given up your credentials and let someone into your organization.

Typically, careful reading of the email will reveal poor enough grammar that will tip you off; however, AI is changing all of that and these attacks are getting very sophisticated. You can sometimes notice nuances in the sender's email address and that of others that might be copied on the email. Regardless, when in doubt, do not click on links and *never* disclose your credentials . . . ever. If it is that important, and you do not answer, the sender will find a way to contact you. Your university has an interest in protecting its network, so they will load and update security software for your computer.

246. Don't get on too many email lists. It is easy to join lots of email lists that will bring you interesting news of your field from inside and outside academia. Like alcohol, email lists should be used in moderation or not at all. Too many, and you waste your morning going through your email rather than paying attention to teaching and research. A good practice is to get a Gmail or similar account just for these sorts of lists. Then, they do not clog your daily email.

247. One last note on email. Answer your email. Not answering email is equivalent to someone talking to you and you not answering. If you are out of the office, put on your out of office reply. The out of office reply should contain when you will return and who can be contacted in your absence. This is common courtesy—use it.

248. Productivity software. Before you invest in expensive software, find out what the university provides for free. These will likely fall into the software categories of:

- Productivity (email, word processing, spreadsheets, etc.)
- Statistics (qualitative, quantitative, modeling, etc.)

- Collaboration (portable documents, video conference, white board, file share, etc.)
- Writing (bibliographic, collaboration tools, etc.)
- Survey administration (both HIPAA and non-HIPAA compliant)
- Business intelligence

If you need software that is not provided for free by the university, it is best to write it into a grant and pay for it that way.

249. Keep up with digital developments. Wikis, blogs, instant voting and feedback, and course management software are four examples. Your students will often know about new computer tools before you or even your IT people do, and they will expect you to know about them and use them.

- Wikis—the term *wiki* comes from Hawaiian and it means to do things quickly. A wiki is software that creates a public text forum that can be edited or added to by anyone with access to the Internet or to a school's local Intranet. Wikis are extremely simple and easy to use by nontechnical people. For example, each student in a class can contribute material to a written discussion, submit homework, or receive information from the instructor or a teaching assistant. Using a wiki for homework discourages plagiarism among students because each student's work is seen by everyone else in the class.
- Wikipedia—Wikipedia (http://www.wikipedia.org) is a large wiki that contains an electronic encyclopedia, much larger than the *Encyclopedia Britannica*, freely available on the Internet. It is a marvelous place to obtain an introduction to almost any topic. Two caveats: Because of its open authorship, Wikipedia can and does sometimes contain errors, and your students may be tempted to plagiarize Wikipedia in their papers. It is wise to check Wikipedia to catch copying.
- Blogs/Vlogs—the term *blog/vlog* comes from *Web/video log*. It refers to websites maintained by one or more individuals who create a diary with the most recent entry shown first rather than last and with the intent of being publicly available rather than private. Blogs/Vlogs are usually interactive so readers can make comments. Blogs/Vlogs can be on any subject, such as the material being covered in a class, politics, or simply personal records. You, as a faculty member, can maintain a blog/vlog for comment by your students and vice versa. These are typically used by influencers.
- Instant feedback and voting—various polling software can be used in the classroom and are an example of instant feedback to gauge the audience's perspective or reaction to a question or position. Using polling is helpful to keep students engaged—online or in person.

- Course management software—used by faculty and students this software is designed to improve communication on what is required in a course and on its content. For a given course, students can find the syllabus, texts required and recommended, assignments, messages from faculty and other students, chat rooms for studying jointly for exams, and they can take exams. They also can be directed to material that expands on the course. Among many on the market, Blackboard, Canvas, and Moodle are perhaps the largest, most available management software packages used by colleges and universities. If you are moving to a new campus, find out which course management software is used there. It is prudent to obtain training on the software before you arrive, as you may be expected to start using it on the first day of class. Remember, your course management system is often the legal record for your course, so treat it as such and ensure that it is updated appropriately.

250. Meetings and digital publications. Become familiar with the digital aspects involved in publishing and presentations at conferences. They're all done by email. Even if you don't write for the electronic journals in your field, you will still use email to:

- Submit your articles (and resubmit revisions)
- Receive review comments
- Receive letters of acceptance
- Receive and send back proof copies

You will find it easiest to set up separate folders for each article. Also, use identification numbers or dates for each version you create so you can keep track of what is current and what is old.

251. Interlibrary loans are quicker and more efficient than they used to be. For example, you can order reprints of journal articles delivered to your email inbox. But you need to know the full reference to get what you want. We recommend *not* giving up going to the library to browse through the stacks where you will find articles and books you didn't know existed. Note that many libraries are going digital, and theirs is a mailing list you want to be on.

252. Use digital libraries if they are available in your field. Many professional organizations, particularly in the sciences, offer full paper access to all their publications, past and present, via the Internet. However, these libraries are not free. Typically, you must be a member of the organization and pay an annual fee. On the other hand, these libraries are so vast and searchable, that the fee is well worth it, whether you are primarily a researcher or a teacher.

253. The "ungettable" article. Sometimes, in your search for the "home run" paper that is going to make the perfect contribution to your literature review, you find that it simply is not available. Your library cannot get it, you cannot get it through interlibrary loan, and you do not belong to a professional organization where you can get it. When all else fails, write to the corresponding author. Most of the time, they will send it to you—after all, they want their work cited.

254. Telecommuting/Work from home (or elsewhere). It is critical that you understand the culture of your department. While many departments may have previously required you to be in your office at least four days a week, the COVID-19 pandemic largely changed that. However, be sure you know. You do not want to be seen as the new person who is never there.

Particularly in your pre-tenure years, time is one of your most precious resources. Telecommuting from home lets you preserve your time and work without interruption. There are certain activities that you *must* be on campus for (meetings, class, etc.), there are also activities that you *want* to be on campus for (collaborating with colleagues, brainstorming sessions, etc.). Otherwise, we suggest, that you create a very nice working space at home (or at the library) where you can work uninterrupted and without distraction. Avoid Watson's Syndrome (Hint 25) of procrastinating.

255. Your website. People who want to know about you and your work, including the 100 powerful people in your field (Hint 2), will first Google your name to find your website so they can learn about you. So will potential employers, peer reviewers of your grant proposals, and even reviewers of articles you submit (if they know or can deduce your name). Clearly, your Web presence should be outstanding.

Unless you have mastered website creation software, you should hire a specialist. It's worth the expense in the long term. Just make sure that you can easily edit it so you are not paying someone every time the site needs to be edited. In some schools, your department may cover this expense or support the development of a limited or skeletal Web presence for you and your work. In the latter case, develop an extensive personal website and link it to the institution's site.

You probably will need to buy a Web presence (domain name), which is easy to do, unless the domain name you prefer is already taken. Even so, you probably can register a similar name. If MarySmith.com is not available, try MaryBSmith.com or ProfMarySmith.com or DrMarySmith.com. Maintaining a domain name is quite inexpensive.

Your site should contain some or all of the following, along with a formal photograph:

- Home page
- Contact information

- A page about your teaching
- Key publications
- Current research projects
- A one-page professional biography (particularly useful for someone to introduce you as a speaker)
- Perhaps a more personal informal biographical narrative
- A list of your consulting clients if you consult
- A link to your full professional CV

An effective alternative is using something like LinkedIn.

256. Your digital visibility. This is a long hint that will include different digital channels for your consideration. Search engine specialists often refer to search engine optimization (SEO), a process to improve website visibility in search engines—this includes mentions of you on other sites such as your university, LinkedIn, X, and so on. Let's say you are a specialist in health informatics who uses innovative technology to facilitate the effective use of medical information. If someone Googles health informatics, you want your work to pop up on the first page, preferably at or near the top. One strategy that can help you accomplish that goal is to start a blog about your work. The Google algorithm tracks how many times people visit a website. If you post items on your topical blog once or twice a week about, say, health informatics, and if you invite comments, you may develop followers. Each time one of them visits your site to read your latest missive, or to post a response, the Google algorithm raises your position by a fraction of space. While it takes many visits for your rank to increase, you have to start somewhere.

- **LinkedIn.** Treat your LinkedIn profile as you would a manuscript abstract. Assume that searching is based on keywords in that profile and that the reader will read no further. Many people have secured lucrative consulting gigs from LinkedIn inquiries. It is also important to make frequent posts to LinkedIn and comment on other posts as this shows you are active and current. Every conference you attend and every paper you present and/or co-author should show up in your feed (include relevant hashtags). If at a conference, include a picture of you presenting. Although this may seem awkward, it is easy to do. Give your phone to someone and ask them to take pictures of you presenting. See if you can get them to video you and then you can post a snippet of that. Some of these will be better quality than others, but that is OK. If you see your collaborators or friends from grad school at the conference, take pictures and post them. Finally, do not complain on LinkedIn about how hard you work or how late you were up grading. Academia is hard work and it is not a 9–5 Monday–Friday job. All academics are in the same boat and no one wants to hear you complain. A note of caution with LinkedIn. There is an option to connect with all of your contacts. Please resist the urge to do so and make your connections intentional and thoughtful.

- **X (formerly Twitter).** Unlike LinkedIn, X is a social networking platform for short, current injections of information that may be of interest to others across broader audiences. X also is used by a lot of influencers and high-profile people (see Hint 2). One of the key differences between X and LinkedIn is the limiting character count of 140 characters in X. Both are excellent social media sites for self-promotion.

- **What is a hashtag and how/why would you use it?** A hashtag is a metadata tag used on social media platforms, such as LinkedIn and X, to make what is written easily discoverable by users interested in a particular topic. Hashtags are written with a # before the word without spaces or punctuation. If you wanted to "advertise" your university at a conference, for example, that would be #University. Regardless, it is important to choose relevant hashtags and keep them simple, yet specific, so #TechnologyTrends is more specific than #Technology. You can also brand yourself with a hashtag that you make up (keep it very simple) and then use that hashtag when you join trending conversations. Don't be shy about including other hashtags in with your posts. Try not to get caught up in the metrics of social media (i.e. likes, shares, etc.)—just do what you do and the appropriate likes and shares will happen, perhaps outside of social media—where they matter most.

257. What is ORCID and why do I need it? ORCID stands for Open Researcher and Contributor ID and provides a unique identifier to permanently connect you to your research. This is especially helpful with common names. Many publishers are now allowing site logins with only an ORCID and then all of your information is auto populated.

258. Build your brand. Building your brand can be done in a number of ways, but the easiest and most far reaching is to do so digitally. Depending on where you are, being in academia can be like running a small business. You are responsible for your business and no one is going to step in to save it. It will be built, survive, and thrive on relationships and hard work. You will need to adapt to identify and obtain funding for your "business." You will spend a large amount of your time trying to obtain funding and managing people. In certain social circles, think about how you introduce yourself. Saying you teach Statistics may turn people off; saying you teach Data Science may fascinate them.

259. Persistence of language. Terms associated with digital media such as *slides* for PowerPoint and *turn the page* for e-books on Kindle and Nook are often vestigial remains from previous technologies. For example, ask undergraduates if they know what "cc", which they see in every email, stands for. Many won't know. (For the record, the answer is "carbon copy," which is to whom copies of memos were sent in the typewriter era.) Such terms are used with the current technology only because they provide a comfortable transition for first adopters. They remain in use because inventing and applying new names is a hassle. In academia, older faculty are more comfortable with the initial terms, but within seven years of introduction of a new term, freshmen no longer identify with the old one.

260. Institutional citizen. As a member of the academic community, you are a citizen of the institution. You have obligations to the institution just as it has obligations to you.

261. Get to know the development people in your school and support them.[2] At most institutions, one or more people on the development department's administrative staff are charged with obtaining endowments and other gifts, maintaining relations with alumni, and so on. Skilled, interactive development office staff can help in obtaining outside funding for you, for your department, and for students, all of which improves your quality of life. Be careful, however; development offices can be horribly inept. Their people are usually underpaid, and in this world you get what you pay for. Many are fund-raisers who know nothing about the academic enterprise or what you do. You will be educating them over and over. You may need to team up with colleagues to get people replaced who are extremely ineffective.

262. Be responsive to the alumni office just as you are to the development office. For many alumni, their college experience is the highlight of their lives, and the old school tie is one of the few things they can flaunt. They like to hear good things about their school because it makes their degree more valuable. If you are asked to write something for the alumni bulletin or give a speech, do it. Alumni can support their old department in a variety of ways. If they know you, they can support you from the outside at crunch time.

263. When you do something noteworthy, let your school's public relations department know, and ask the staff to publicize it. When you publish a book, win a prize, get elected to a professional society office, or do something in the community, get public relations into the act. It is one way for a lot of your colleagues across campus to find out what a wonderful person you are. (They may even remember it at promotion time!) It also gives you an opportunity to brag to your chairperson and the people in your department without being obnoxious about it.

264. Communicating your field to the public. Those who can clearly communicate ideas from their discipline to the public hold an important place in our society. If you develop this skill, you can become a *public intellectual*. Some highly successful public intellectuals have included astronomer Carl Sagan, who had a television series, *Cosmos,* and Neil deGrasse Tyson, who relaunched *Cosmos.* Listed by your school's PR department as an expert in your field, you can expect local (and sometimes national) media to ask for your comments. If you are good on TV, you will be asked about all kinds of topics, many beyond your expertise. Be careful to not pontificate on areas you know next to nothing about.

265. The Faculty Senate in most institutions provides a forum. Faculty are elected to the senate, usually by people in their department or their school. If elected, it provides a way for you to communicate with the higher levels of administration on matters important to you and to your department. Election to the Senate also increases your visibility. Be aware, however, that Faculty Senate work can eat up a large amount of your time. Our advice, therefore, is if you are asked to run, do so, providing you are tenured, and your school's Senate is not a collection of malcontents who are ignored by the administration.

266. Service. The party line is that a junior professor seeking tenure should do well in research, teaching, and service, but they are not equal in value. Service is the least important. One university president admonished new faculty members to earn an A in research, a B in teaching, and a D in service.

While service can include service to your community or city, and service to your discipline nationally, it usually involves serving on faculty committees. Do your share. Avoid being labeled a bad citizen, but do not extend yourself excessively.

Serving on some committees can be a time sump. An example is the institutional review board (Hint 142), where you have to read every research proposal, including student proposals, with a fine-tooth comb. A good department chair or dean will protect you against such committee assignments until you have tenure. If you are uncertain about the time required for various committees, ask around.

Be sure to avoid service that takes time and drags you into faculty politics. For example, don't get elected to the Faculty Executive Committee or the Faculty Senate until you are tenured. Under no circumstances should you serve on a committee that is rewriting by-laws until you are tenured as a full professor.

DEPARTMENT CHAIR

Department chairs will seem to be lofty people to you, having a job you think you should aspire to, but it's not quite all wine and roses.

267. Never, never become a department chair, even an acting department chair, unless you are a tenured full professor. Yes, it will reduce your teaching load. Yes, it will give you visibility. Yes, you will be the first person contacted by an outside firm seeking a consultant. No, it will not confer power on you. The job carries with it some onerous burdens. First and foremost, most department chairs do less research and publish less while in that position than they would as a faculty member. Thus, you are producing less portable wealth per year (Hint 95), and you are reducing your chances of tenure or of promotion. The service you perform does not get you tenure. Don't feel flattered if the job is offered and you are pressured by the dean to accept it (a dean pressuring you when you are not a tenured full professor does not have your back . . . and will not have your back if you take the position). What is really going on is that the dean has no other viable candidate who is willing to do it. If you must accept, realize you are in the same bargaining position as a new hire. The dean wants you badly, so use the opportunity to obtain something in return. Besides a big fat administrative stipend (all of that heartache has to be worth your time), if you are untenured and accept the job, make sure that it is subject to the condition that you will be reviewed for tenure in the next academic year if you are ready. Do not accept the job of chair if you are not ready to be promoted to tenure. Be clear beforehand that you will resign the chair's job if the agreement is broken, and if it is (as is sometimes the case) follow through. As the advertisement says, deans operate on the principle of, "Promise them anything, but give them . . ."

268. Be aware that the powers of a department chair are few. One of us wrote down the following seven absolute powers of department chair he had at a particular university:

- The right to attend meetings of the department chairs with the dean
- The right to chair meetings of the department
- The right to interview candidates for staff positions
- The right (subject to a few side conditions) to select which classes he would teach and at which times
- The right to approve (or disapprove) student petitions
- The right to greet outside visitors to the department
- The right to resign as chair

269. The role of conflict in the job. You will spend a considerable amount of your time solving problems brought to you by your faculty colleagues that they clearly should/could have solved on their own. The faculty will also want you to obtain goodies for them (space, computers, research money, reduced teaching loads, and on and on). On the other hand, the dean will want you to act as a first-line manager whose main role is to keep the "troublemakers" down so they don't get out of hand. "Troublemakers" in academia are often those who have the courage to speak out, ask questions, hold people accountable, and call out wrongs that have been done.

The job is best characterized by these lines from Gilbert and Sullivan's *Gondoliers*:

> But the privilege and pleasure
> That we treasure beyond measure
> Is to run little errands for the Ministers of State!

270. Leadership. As a faculty member you will learn a lot about bad management by observing the various chairs, deans, and higher administrators. You will feel that any dolt could do better than they do, and you will often be right. At some point, however, management may become real for you if you are asked to become a department chair or an associate dean. Now you must provide leadership and avoid the traps your predecessors fell into. Management is a discipline you can study and learn. Those people in the business school really do know something, and what they know is leadership. Like teaching, leadership is a learnable art.

271. Dealing with student problems. If you do become department chair, know that most students who come into your office do so while in crisis. They are unhappy about a grade. They want to be exempted from a course or an examination. They need to explain they did not cheat even though their term paper was identical word for word to one submitted by another student the year before. You are the end of the line for them. You cannot throw them out. You need to listen and be firm but sympathetic at the same time. It takes a strong stomach and a feeling for people.

272. The redeeming social value of being chair. Despite the forgoing caveats, being a department chair does have redeeming social values. If you have a vision of where you think the future of the department lies, you can use your moral suasion as chair to move people in the direction you believe is right. Notice we use the term *moral suasion*, not power. You need to develop a constituency for your ideas. In academia, Theory X management (I tell, you do) does not apply. Japanese Theory Z management (nothing happens until a consensus is reached) is the appropriate model.

273. Don't stay in the chair position too long. If you do, you become a victim of your past decisions. You become locked into doing what you did before, whether it is still the appropriate thing to do or not. Fortunately, unlike industry, you can keep pace if you step down and work for someone who previously worked for you. When you step down, don't second-guess your successors on every little point. They, like you before them, need all the help they can get. Also, be aware that you are now faculty and no longer department chair. You may find yourself needing to follow some of the policies that you put in place that seemed reasonable when you were chair and now seem unreasonable to you as a faculty member.

274. You can go home again—retreat rights. When you accept a new job, either internal or external to your institution, you may have retreat rights. That is, under some circumstances you can go back to the position you held previously. The people who do this the most leave academia to take major government jobs such as economic adviser to the US president. Retreat rights also apply to administrators (e.g., department chairs, deans, presidents), who typically go back to being faculty members. The policy also applies to research projects, pregnancy, and other situations. Typically, academic institutions let you take a leave of absence for non-university jobs for up to two years and will not extend it beyond that.

TRAVEL AND CONFERENCES

Although you can keep in contact with your field through reading books and journals, corresponding by email, and hearing lecturers that come to your department, what you learn is limited. Dating back to the Royal Society of London in the 17th century, academics travel to conferences to expand their horizons by finding out and discussing what is new. We suggest negotiating a conference travel budget when you negotiate your job.

275. Professional travel. One of the best aspects of academia is that professors travel, subsidized by employer and grant funding, to interesting places and they meet interesting people.[3] Travel is a major fringe benefit, but the amount of travel varies by field and by institution. In most fields, one or more major meetings a year take place at the national and regional levels. Despite financial stringencies, most institutions pay your way if you are on the program or involved in recruiting (usually restricted to senior faculty). Furthermore, each meeting is scheduled in a different location. Since it is easier to win approval for a short trip than it is for long trips, take the opportunity to attend nearby meetings whenever they occur.

For full-time graduate students, meetings are a little more difficult to attend because little funding is usually available and few graduate students are personally wealthy. Yes, students pay lower (usually much lower) registration fees, share rooms at a Day's Inn or Motel Six (although various social factors are making this less and less likely), and for reasonable distances can carpool. Still, it is a financial stretch. If you're the best doctoral student close to a degree, you may be designated as your program's candidate for the doctoral consortium. You then must compete with other candidates for an available slot. If you win that lottery, you may get most or all of your expenses paid.

276. Attend conferences. Conferences in your professional specialty are held all the time and become a significant part of your academic life that begins when you are a graduate student. Some are small, others huge. You should attend conferences whenever possible because of the following advantages:

- You present your work to knowledgeable leaders who provide valuable feedback.
- You can hear and meet many of the 100 powerful people (Hint 2).
- You learn about new ideas, the hot new topics, and, if you're astute, what is now passé. Like Sherlock Holmes in the *Hound of the Baskervilles*, you learn from what is not being barked at the meeting.
- You make new friends (the real kind, not the Facebook kind), and you can check out which colleges and universities are good places for professors and which are not.
- You learn about the job market and who needs faculty because schools recruit at larger conferences. If you are job hunting as a soon-to-be PhD or looking for a better position, comparison shop just as recruiters comparison shop candidates.
- If there is a publisher's book fair, you find out about new books and texts.
- You can learn about funding opportunities.

277. Choosing your conferences. Choose conferences that relate closely to your dissertation, research, or teaching interests. Most fields use email listserves to publicize meetings. You should get on their mailing lists.

At a national conference, the papers are more interesting but you may feel overwhelmed. Unless they are within driving distance, national conferences tend to be more expensive (travel, registration, hotel). Regional and graduate student conferences are lower cost and lower level and may not be as overwhelming.

You apply to present at most conferences with an abstract, due well in advance. Prepare it carefully. If you're presenting work from your dissertation, edit the abstract so it applies to the conference theme. Create an abstract that grabs the program committee's interest. Good abstracts are hard to write. Pay attention to them, and don't toss them off in an hour.

Be aware that conferences use up a chunk of your time. If your abstract is accepted, you will be asked to submit a paper, which again is due well before the conference. If the paper passes peer review and is accepted, you may have a publication (many conferences publish conference proceedings). Still, you will need to proofread the paper, obtain funding to go, find people to cover your classes while you are away, spend as much as a day traveling in each direction, and spend additional days at the meeting. We won't even mention the hassles at airports.

278. Your conference presentation. Rehearse your presentation, preferably in front of your friends and colleagues, before you leave for the conference. Most likely, your paper will be one of several in a session. You will be allocated 15 minutes, with perhaps 5 minutes for a senior person (called a discussant) to give you instant feedback.

Some conference presentations are superb, and you learn from them. Others drone on and on and on. Your own performance will be judged by your audience. Stay within your time limit, and be at least as clear as when you teach a class.

If you are comfortable with presentation software (Hint 113), use it. Show only your main points and charts and resist the urge to clog the slides with font that is too small.

Don't worry if one or two people walk out when you start your talk. When sessions are simultaneous, people sometimes switch to another paper being presented at the same time as yours. However, if many people walk out while you talk, it's a bad sign.

279. Protect your intellectual capital while traveling. You can publish your research findings in a journal after you have presented a paper on them at a conference. Be careful, however, not to present creative initial speculations and hypotheses you are not yet ready to publish. They can be stolen by unscrupulous members of your audience.

280. Working while conferencing. Attending conferences is essential to your professional development and intellectual growth. However, if you are not answering email or doing any work while at a conference, you will quickly get behind. Put your out of office message on your email to help manage your delayed replies—we suggest setting your out of office message for four hours later than when you actually return to the office to give you time to get caught up. This does not absolve you from your work while conferencing, it only manages expectations for your replies. Students and your chair, however, should be responded to as soon as possible.

281. Drew's rule of conference redundancy. You can cite a previously published finding or one you presented at an earlier conference in a new and different context. But don't overdo it. Here is a good rule of thumb: If you found a correlation (a number between 0 and 1), multiply it by 10. That's how many years you can still discuss it.

For example, one of us discovered and reported a correlation of 0.91 between (a) the prestige of graduate mathematics departments and (b) the rate at which their faculty published in the discipline's most highly cited journals. He was asked to discuss this finding at several conferences and accepted the last such invitation . . . nine years later.

GRIEVANCES

There comes a time in the life of students and faculty when they whine about the injustice of it all. As an academic you need to know about grievance procedures.

282. You may be involved in a student grievance at some point in your academic career. We are a litigious society, fueled in part by a supply of lawyers and in part by demand for equal treatment under the law. Fortunately, most universities and colleges have grievance procedures to handle disputes. We estimate that the chance of your being involved in a student grievance sometime during your academic career is 50 percent. Typically, these disputes are over grades, results of examinations, acts of cheating, and the like. Sometimes they are the result of delusions by students about their abilities. Other times they are the results of behavior on your part that a student perceives as insulting or demeaning.

283. Faculty grievances. Never underestimate the actions of another colleague who might be jealous of your success. Faculty file grievances against other faculty—faculty that work together. Be aware. Unless there is something egregious, we do not recommend filing a grievance against a colleague. This never ends well for the grievance filer when the faculty member is found "innocent."

284. Sexual harassment. In the last decade incidents of sexual harassment have grown as a basis for complaints. You may wind up as the originator or the recipient of such a complaint. The source may be a student, a staff member, or another faculty member. Remember that harassment complaints can lead to litigation in court. Your institution may or may not be supportive. If it isn't, you can wind up spending large amounts on lawyers and court fees. The best strategy is preventive. Here are a few things you can do to protect yourself:

- Know and obey your institution's rules on harassment.
- Know what the procedures are for the offended party.
- Never meet on your own with a student of either sex behind a closed door.[4]
- Never meet with a faculty member of either sex behind a closed door.
- Never use language or examples that can be construed as sexually offensive, if even remotely. If in doubt, don't say it.

285. Faculty rarely volunteer to serve on the grievance committee. It is not a pleasant duty. This results in members often being appointed to this committee when they are not appropriate for other vacancies, and they do not have the experience or skills of judges or dispute professionals. Like most judicial proceedings, the results involve a certain element of chance. Committees often fudge the outcome, particularly if the grievance is framed in a "she said, he said" form. Thus, even if you are completely in the right in a dispute, try to avoid using this committee. Furthermore, as a young faculty member, avoid serving on this committee if at all possible.

286. You may become the grievant against your institution. Disputes can arise over such issues as: tenure; sabbatical entitlements; teaching loads; outrageous treatment by department chairs or deans; salaries; discrimination because of age, gender, or ethnicity; and more. The bad news is that many people will remember the incident negatively even when you win (Hint 283).

DEALING WITH MYTHS

When you talk with family, friends, and others who do not work in academia, don't be surprised to discover that they believe some of the standard myths about professors. The following hints deal with two of them.

287. Myth 1: Faculty enjoy lots of free time. "I envy all the free time you have. You mean you actually get paid for working 12 hours a week?" They may also tell you that old joke; Question: What does a professor say at the end of the work week? Answer: Thank goodness it's Tuesday.

Actually, most professors work well over 40 hours per week, and that includes not only time spent on campus, but also time working at home in the evenings and on weekends. If your department offers courses to students who are employed full-time, you will be on campus some nights until 9:00 or 10:00.

288. Myth 2: Faculty's political leanings. "All professors are political Leftists. Our universities are controlled by radicals and liberals."

Many professors are either conservative or middle of the road. You will discover that when it comes to changing their own behavior, your colleagues are unusually conservative and move very slowly. They follow Frank H. T. Rhodes's sardonic assertion "Never, under any circumstance, do something for the first time."[5]

NOTES

1 In some places, computing is outsourced. However, it requires lots of local staff to actually run the IT center.

2 *Development* is an old-fashioned term. Many of the larger schools use the more fashionable word *advancement*. Ironically, most advancement campaigns begin with a retreat for faculty.

3 Make sure that you fully understand what is required of you to travel and exactly what the university or a grant will cover. For example, if you do not have a travel request approved, you may not be reimbursed.

4 Some of our colleagues believe this advice is too stringent. They argue that when a student requests privacy, it calls for a closed door. We disagree. Privacy can be achieved as easily by walking with the student to a quiet food area or public space.

5 The late Frank H. T. Rhodes was President Emeritus of Cornell University. He made this statement at the 1997 opening of the Keck Graduate Institute. He referred to it as the cardinal law of academic governance. (Reported as paraphrased by David Drew who was in attendance.)

Chapter 13

Equity and Values

Hint 289 Although you may hear that universities are trying to narrow the various diversity and opportunity gaps . . . the changes may be seen as negligible.

We want to help the reader who belongs to a marginalized group (or more than one, intersectionality) to navigate higher education and to enjoy your best life in the best job. In this chapter, we discuss equity and values, and provide some of the recent history and debates in higher education about these issues.

Whereas portions of this book take a lighthearted view of many aspects of academe, in this chapter we take a more serious tone.

We are opposed to all forms of discrimination. Our main recommendation, which is reflected in several hints: if you are a member of an underrepresented group, or if you simply prize fairness, use your research skills to find out whether or not a potential institutional home is supportive of these values.

As a matter of historical background, in the 1960s, affirmative action was introduced under the Civil Rights Act of 1964, followed by a Presidential Executive Order in 1965. Within about 30 years, the Supreme Court enacted changes to the practice of affirmative action and race could no longer be a determining factor in student admissions or employment. As of the printing of this edition, the Supreme Court is still hearing cases related to race-based admissions and employment decisions.

Unlike affirmative action, which was intended to be a remedial measure to address historical discrimination, diversity, equity, and inclusion (DEI) initiatives are intended to create environments where *everyone* feels valued, respected, included, and supported. While the origins of DEI are rooted in the 1960s at a time when societal movements and legal changes began to reshape the corporate world, it gained significant momentum in the mainstream in the late 20th and early 21st century with evolving societal attitudes, legal developments, globalization, and activism.

As we close out the first quarter of this century (the period in which this book is being written), we find the diversity climate changing, to the point where some schools and colleges have banned books and abolished or severely restricted classroom discussion. In recent years, a groundswell of backlash against DEI began, citing issues such as real or perceived reverse discrimination, political polarization, creating a culture of tokenism, and others. This movement has joined forces with politicians trying to dictate what can and cannot be taught in classrooms.

From this short historical narrative, one wonders how far we have really come in creating environments where *everyone* feels valued, respected, included, and supported. Many students from marginalized groups have found that creating an affinity group within the university, or within a major in the university (for example, Latinas in Engineering) can provide them with both friendship and support. To that end, we strongly recommend that in your job search you pay attention to the mission, vision, and values of the university, school, and department. They should all be aligned with one another, and they should be something that you can embrace, defend, and drive. While aligning your values to a university has been commonplace in faith-based universities, it is only recently that this has had such a strong foothold in secular educational environments.

289. The continuing goal. Although you may hear that universities are trying to narrow the various diversity and opportunity gaps, if graduate students are not choosing to enter academia, the changes may be seen as negligible and also may take a long time to be achieved.

290. Variations among institutions. Diversity focus varies greatly among institutions.[1] Our experience is that most universities are focused on narrowing the ethnic, gender, and sexual orientation opportunity gaps. When considering an offer, and even when making an application, try to find out whether the institution you are considering as your future intellectual home shows a genuine openness and commitment to supporting and mentoring *all* junior faculty. A massive study of attempts by universities to diversify their faculty concluded, "Campuses with greatest gains had explicitly connected their efforts to their educational mission and had implemented multiple strategies to improve the recruitment and selection process with regard to [underrepresented minority] candidates."[2]

291. Aligning values. It is critical that the values of the university are aligned with your values. While this is true at many universities, faith-based universities tend to be more explicit about their expectations around values alignment. The other end of the values spectrum is public universities. Due to the public nature of these universities and their being funded with public tax dollars, they are also more likely to be silent on some of the more controversial areas of values alignment. For example, their values statement might be centered around valuing collaboration and innovation. In private universities, the values can be heavily driven by both board members' perspectives and faculty perspectives.

Regardless of where you wind up, it is critical that you figure out if your values are in alignment with those of your department and the university. If not, then your daily life may be uncomfortable and the road to tenure and promotion will certainly be rocky. One of the authors tells a story about a very well-meaning dean who pulled her aside during an interview at a faith-based institution and told her that there were no tenured faculty of her faith (but there were a lot of students of various faiths), and while she was qualified, she might want to rethink moving forward in the process. She respectfully removed herself from the remainder of the interview process.

292. Assessing colleagues and deans. When looking for your first job or changing jobs, try to assess how open and supportive an institution is, as well as, to the best of your ability, the openness and support of your future department colleagues and your future dean. As we said in Hint 219, don't assume you can outwait a bad dean.

Given a Hobson's choice, it is better to take a position at the institution of your second choice if it has a supportive culture (even if its academic reputation is slightly lower) with better aligned values in which you can flourish, than at your top choice if you conclude you will encounter forms of discrimination that impede growth.

293. Accommodations for students. Some types of disabilities require that you give your students certain accommodations. You should be notified of these through your disability support services office, or another similar office. For example, you may be asked to give more time on examinations to students with dyslexia or other learning disabilities. Accommodation is not only good policy, it is the law (Americans With Disabilities Act of 1990). Once you have been notified of the accommodation, you must provide it. However, if a student discloses a reason to you for an accommodation, you should direct them to the disability support services office as this is the official notification point for student accommodations. Remember, this is protected health information and should never be discussed with others (see Hint 130 on FERPA).

294. Accommodations for you. If you have a disability or have other reasons for accommodations, carefully study how a prospective employer addresses your need for accommodations. Some institutions are more welcoming than others.

NOTES

1 A respected guide for institutions that want to increase diversity in a meaningful way is Daryl G. Smith, *Diversity's Promise for Higher Education: Making It Work,* third edition (Baltimore, MD: Johns Hopkins University Press, 2020).

2 José F. Moreno, D. G. Smith, A. R. Clayton-Pedersen, S. Parker, D. H. Teraguchi (2006) "The revolving door for underrepresented minority faculty in higher education." *The James Irvine Foundation Campus Diversity Initiative Evaluation Project* (2006), Association of American Colleges and Universities, pp. 7–8.

Chapter 14

Personal Considerations

Hint 300 Learn time management.

PERSONAL CONSIDERATIONS

The hints in this chapter refer to your actions as an individual. They range from advice about time management to observations about how your interests and career directions might change over time to ethical challenges you might confront.

295. Learn new things over time. Universities are notorious for not spending money on faculty development; their administrators assume that because you earned a PhD you have learned all you will ever need to know. They are not consumers of their own educational product. Actually, you know the most about your field the week you take the prelims (or comps or quals) for the PhD. Thereafter, you tend to specialize and learn more and more about the narrower and narrower subfield you work in. But it is unfortunately true that fields change over time. Some subspecialties are mined out, and new results become ever more difficult to obtain. Other subspecialties make rapid strides that require you to learn new methodologies and become aware of a flood of literature. Some new technologies or tools, such as generative AI, come along and change the research skills you need. If something new is important to your research, try to get your department to spring for some education. It may be a short course offered by the leading expert in the field or a tutorial offered at a professional meeting. If the time needed is sufficiently long, arrange your next sabbatical at one of the centers where the new knowledge is being developed.

296. Sequential careers. As a graduate student you may aspire to be the best professor of French or Biology or Sociology ever known, but the reality is that your interests and your circumstances will likely change. New topics arise, subfields stagnate or disappear, colleagues ask you to collaborate and cooperate, doctoral students ask you to serve on their committee on a topic, you start teaching a new course, or you take your sabbatical in a new environment.

In talking with your professors while you are a graduate student, and later with your colleagues, you will find that some well-respected individuals reached their current position serendipitously. For example, one of the authors of this book was a lead programmer at a famous university, a senior analyst for a Washington think tank, a statistician, a professor in the Social Sciences, and for a number of years, a dean. Another worked as a scientific editor, a large-scale systems researcher, department chair, and wrote first papers in three different fields. Yet another was a nurse, then an elementary school teacher, then worked for the state, before settling into academia where her research has spanned across multiple disciplines. Each career change involved its own logic and leverage points. For all of us, what we learned previously proved to be a foundation for the stages that followed. Do your work and your leverage point will be an easy retrospective find.

Bottom line: Don't be afraid to tackle new directions. You can change what you do.

297. Being an expert witness. One day the phone will ring or you will receive an email and you will be asked by a lawyer to be an expert witness. The attorney will tell you that all you need to do is help prepare the technical material in your specialty (which is fun) and to appear in court to swear to your findings. An ethical attorney will offer you a fixed fee or a fixed hourly rate rather than ask you to bet on the contingency that your side will win. It looks like easy money, but it isn't really that simple. The legal culture is different from your field's culture. You will need to bridge the two-culture gap; lawyers won't and can't, so you must teach the attorneys about your field. If you are a scientist, you will blanch at the low level of proof offered in court cases, and you will be appalled at the level of statistics being cited. When you do get to court, you will find you spend much of your time waiting around. Waiting is not bad; you are getting paid a premium for every hour spent in court. When it does come time to take the stand, your side's lawyer will lead you through a carefully rehearsed set of questions. Then the fun begins. The other side's lawyer will cross-examine you. The operative word is *cross*. That lawyer will try to find inconsistencies in what you said. The opposing side will try to twist your words to be favorable to its client. The other attorney will try to impugn your expertise, your honesty, your veracity. You can come out with a very jaundiced view of jurisprudence. The whole process will eat up a large chunk of your time, and if you are an untenured professor, remember that the income carries with it a big cost in opportunity—the time lost working on your research. The work for a court case is almost never the basis of something publishable. Tenure committees view being an expert witness as a public service or consulting income, not professional work no matter how complex or visible the case. If you do become a regularly employed expert witness, your initial choice of sides can quickly become permanent. If you are hired, say, by plaintiffs seeking psychic pain and suffering awards in auto accident cases one day, you will not credibly be able to represent an insurance company defendant the next.

You should conduct your analyses with integrity and report your findings with candor; even though this ethical approach may cost you some expert witness income. If the attorney doesn't like your findings from your background work, they won't ask you to testify in court and may not hire you for the next case.

298. Whistle-blowing. Every so often you will observe a situation in your department or your institution that you believe is not right. The situation might involve overpromising or underperforming by an administrator, or downright dishonesty (e.g., changing a grade you gave or taking bribes). A natural response is to become a whistle-blower. It is a response we respect and is in keeping with academic freedom.

Be aware, however, that whistle-blowing involves considerable risk. Yes, there is satisfaction in speaking up in a meeting or writing a letter to the local newspaper exposing the unethical deed. But the people involved will try to squelch you or retaliate if they can, even if silently. They can remember at tenure time, they can try to have you fired, they can try to ruin your reputation. None of these outcomes is desirable. If the infraction is minor, we recommend you note it in your head for future reference. If it is major, start talking with people you absolutely trust. Build a coalition rather than being out front on your own. Unfortunately, it is often the whistle-blower who winds up changing jobs and not the person or people accused of the wrong-doing.

299. Don't be a penny-ante thief. It may be awfully tempting to put personal correspondence in official envelopes, to use department staff to type your private letters, or to make personal calls to foreign countries, but don't. And don't use department funds to buy software or journal subscriptions to support your consulting practice. To paraphrase Abe Lincoln, you can get away with some of it all the time, and you can get away with all of it some of the time, but you can't get away with all of it all the time. Don't develop a reputation of being someone who only takes not gives, of not having ethical respect for your colleagues or your institution.

300. Learn time management. First, finish reading this book. Then determine your work priorities and try as best you can to match your time commitments to those priorities.

The model of an academic having large blocks of time at work to think deeply about a problem is not real and may never have been. Your time on campus is fragmented. You get interrupted for teaching, office hours, supervising dissertations, phone calls, keeping up with email, research, writing, publishing, and more, all of which are important or mandatory. You barely have time to be collegial (Hint 226).

If you are overloaded, use time management tools. The simplest is the calendar that comes with email software. Keep a record not only of your appointments and your teaching commitments, but also your interruptions. An analysis will show when you can combine repetitive interruptions and when you can undertake reading, research, and professional activities. Typically, calendars on enterprise email are open for viewing, even if not at the detail level. We recommend blocking time on your calendar for focused work time. This way, someone looking to schedule a meeting will work around that time period.

Learn to say no. One of our colleagues, who published well over 30 books in their career, said: "If you write only a page a day, that's a book a year." For more, read Alan Lakein's marvelous, short guide to time management.[1]

301. The meaning of your work will change over time. Whether you pursue multiple careers or stay in one subject area at one location, you will find that what your work means to you will change over time (Hint 296). When you start out, you will naturally want to publish and carry forward the work that began with your dissertation. You will be learning more about teaching and becoming involved in institutional service. Over your initial years, your self-concept of your mix of teaching, research, and service will change. This shift occurs because of the institution(s) you work for, the assignments you receive, your level of success at each component of your mix, and the students you deal with.

302. Completion time. No matter how long you think it will take to:

- Write a paper based on your research
- See the article you just submitted in print
- Complete a research project
- Prepare a new course
- Prepare for a session of a course you gave previously

it will take longer . . . much longer.

Especially when you first start out, we recommend that you have a table of your activities with a time commitment. Try not to exceed 100 percent; however, that is near impossible to do and maintain the kind of productivity that will earn you good teaching evaluations, tenure, and promotion. A more realistic effort might be 150 percent, mostly because however long you think something will take, it will likely take twice as long.

Optimist or pessimist? Wide-eyed optimists always think the task will be completed on time, while mildly realistic optimists think the task will take their estimated time plus 10 percent, and pessimists assume the delay is at least 50 percent on average. Better to be a pessimist and have extra time on your hands than an optimist and constantly be late. Plus, this helps establish you as someone who always meets deadlines (Hint 158).

Corollary: Even if you add these delay times to your estimate, it will still take longer than that.

303. Failure is an opportunity. Robert F. Kennedy said, "Forgive your enemies. But remember their names."

Our goal in these hints is to facilitate your success and prevent failure. We wish you the best: that you complete your PhD, secure an appointment, achieve tenure, and, in due time, are promoted to full professor.

If you fail, try to learn from the experience. Most scholars experienced one or more failures along the way, and the great world-class scholars turned those failures into opportunities.

If you fail, say, to achieve tenure the first time, see what you can learn from the experience. Do you need to publish more articles or improve your teaching? Did you find out that one of your colleagues cannot be trusted? Each of these is a valuable lesson.

Try not to become consumed with anger and regret. Regret about yesterday only degrades your own experience today. Enjoy today, and look to the future.

NOTE

1 Alan Lakein, *How to Get Control of Your Time and Life* (New York, NY: Penguin Signet, 1974).

Chapter 15
Your Health

Hint 310 Addictions and **Hint 316** Meditation.

You must stay healthy to continue to hold down the academic job that you sought for so long. Unless you keep your health, you can take ill, fatigue easily, or feel all sorts of aches and pains. While you cannot escape conditions to which you might be genetically predisposed, there is a lot that you can do to mitigate risk, decrease stress, and enjoy your academic life. In this chapter, we offer hints about some of the issues you can encounter and what you can do to maintain balance and health. These hints are based on our experience. They are not intended as medical advice. We are neither physicians nor health specialists, but rather experienced academics who have lived through stressful job situations that could have been avoided. We give you hints with the lessons we have learned—if only we knew then what we know now!

304. Mental and physical wellness. Be prepared to be at odds with yourself and your environment. Your mental and physical well-being may take a beating both while you are awake and while you are asleep. Just when you think you have it under control, self-doubt creeps in. Learn to lean into these feelings with mediation, healthy nutrition, and exercise—success is right around the corner (see various hints in this chapter)

305. Avoid stress. Although we go into academia because we think it involves little stress, that's a legend that is not true. If you're junior and nontenured, you can expect that obtaining tenure will be the most intense, stressful experience you will face in your entire career—but it really does not need to be surrounded by the fury and frenzy that you hear about (Hint 182). You will be wondering whether you will be awarded tenure (it is never a slam dunk) and worrying about what you will do if you aren't. Furthermore, stress is not necessarily over once you become tenured, although it is usually diminished. Of course, if you are a type A personality (impatient, insecure about yourself, competitive, aggressive, and rarely relax) you add your own level of stress to that which may already exist.

Stress caused by the following also awaits you from outside academe:

- Money—for most professors, unless your family or you are really well off, when you start your academic career you will face the problem of managing much more salary than you ever had as a graduate student. Although the salary may seem princely, you will still need to pay off your student debts, and you will make considerably less than senior professors. The monthly check may never seem to go far enough. You must learn how to manage your money.
- Family responsibilities—most people receive their PhDs between the ages of 25 and 35. If you don't already have a spouse or partner, these are often the years when you take on family responsibilities, emotional and financial, in addition to your nontrivial workload.

- Parents—as people live longer, your parents and grandparents will need care, and the responsibilities for that care can become yours. This may be on top of your becoming a parent. Affectionately called the sandwich generation.

The problems of money, family responsibilities, and parents don't go away even after tenure. Whether you are tenured or not, you will experience stress from within your institution. For example, a bad dean, a school in financial crisis, a department riven by politics, and outside political attacks on the university all contribute to stress. You will also feel transient stresses, such as the potential repercussions from a student you failed or from the rejection of a paper you thought was great or the stress of a rejected grant application— meaning that you now have to pick up a course you have never taught before. Sometimes you need a little humor to carry you through a tough time. Our favorite story about academic humor dates back to the 1960s. The student protests of that decade began with the "Free Speech" movement at the University of California, Berkeley (UCB). The UCB Chancellor was one of the 20th century's great academic leaders and higher education scholars, Clark Kerr. The students saw Kerr as the establishment symbol of everything they were protesting against. That year, Ronald Reagan was running for governor. He attacked both the protestors and Kerr! He portrayed Kerr as a dangerous radical. Reagan said that, if he were elected governor, he would appoint University of California Regents who would fire Kerr. He was elected and, indeed, appointed new Regents who fired Kerr. That day, Clark Kerr called a press conference and said, "I leave this campus with the same emotion as when I first arrived at Berkeley as a college freshman: fired with enthusiasm."

306. Breaks. Regardless of whether you are a graduate student or a faculty member there are no breaks (spring, summer, holiday, etc.), only time to catch up on things. When you take vacation time, put on your out of office reply and take your vacation as that will be the only time you truly get a break. Learn to set appropriate limits on how many thankless tasks you are willing to do. Academia can be harsh—listen to your body and remember to take time for yourself.

307. Start a health and fitness program if you are not already involved in one. As academics, we take the written word seriously. Therefore, we suggest you begin by reading one or two of the many excellent books about health. Use well-established books, rather than the latest faddish one on magic exercises or fantastic diets. Talk with people in your school's health service or athletic department for specific recommendations.

308. Exercise. The establishment (public health officials and the medical community) is always after us to exercise regularly, and the establishment is right. If you're a couch potato who goes from the computer to the television and then to bed, find a half hour every day for some form of exercise, preferably aerobics.[1] For example,

- Walk a half hour every day
- Ride a bike
- Jog
- Swim

If you enjoy a form of exercise, you are more likely to continue and make it a lifelong habit. If you prefer, or you need to stay disciplined, use a gym. Often, institutions offer exercise programs/facilities for faculty. After all, if you cannot devote 30 minutes to yourself, something is definitely imbalanced in your life. One of us consistently recommends exercise to all students who complain they are lost, cannot think, cannot write, are depressed, or a myriad of other maladies. They give the student a reprieve from meetings and work for a month to establish an exercise routine. The students come back happier and significantly more productive.

309. Daily gratitude journaling. Practice some form of daily gratitude journaling to help overcome challenges and move on. This practice will also let you appreciate how far you have come.

310. Addictions. We discuss three addictions here: nicotine, drugs, and alcohol, but this information also applies to other addictions, such as being an email junkie.

Tobacco use of any kind (smoking, chewing, vaping) is something you should try to avoid. We know this is easier for us to say than for you to do, but try to get help to reduce your reliance on these substances. There are a lot of tobacco cessation programs available. Shop around until you find a program that works for you. The cost of the tobacco products that you don't use will more than pay for the program. A note on vaping: Many tobacco-free campuses have caught on and have included vaping or e-cigarettes in the category of banned substances on campus.

Drugs and alcohol. We won't go into detail on drugs or alcohol here. Suffice it to say that if you are addicted to either or both, it can:

- Be successful grounds for firing you even if you are tenured. Obtaining another job will be difficult.
- Reduce your research output, particularly for tenure.
- Be nearly impossible to hide for long periods of time. You're a public person (Hint 227) who is observed by all around you. Some of your students or colleagues will pick up on it, and word will get around.

311. Drink water. You would be amazed at how drinking water will perk you up mid-day and increase your overall stamina. In addition to keeping you hydrated, water acts as a transportation vehicle for nutrition (see the next two hints). It further detoxifies your body, clearing out a lot of impurities that can impact your ability to think clearly, thereby improving cognitive function. Water also helps with weight management and cardiovascular health. The recommended amount of water is one-half of your weight in ounces. So, if you weigh 150 pounds you should be drinking 75 ounces of water, or about two-thirds of a gallon daily.

312. Learning about nutrition. Eating nutritiously has a host of benefits. The food that we eat now is not the same as the food that we were eating 20 years ago. Food processing has changed and led to many allergies and weight issues that never used to exist. There are several good video documentaries on food processing that will help educate you (search for "food processing documentary"). Of course, if you specialize in nutrition, you already know all of this and can likely move on. Once you have watched these, start eliminating certain foods little by little—all at once will set you up for failure.

313. Benefits of good nutrition. Much like the benefits of water, the benefits of good nutrition enhance your performance and your mental health. Think of good nutrition like gasoline for your body. You would not put second rate gasoline in your precious car, or go 20,000 miles without changing the oil, or force it to run on empty, but yet we demand that of our bodies. Studies of people who live to be quite old, (including those over 100) consistently find common nutrition elements. Nutrition recommendations could easily yield a book much larger than this one. Read one or two books on healthy nutrition. It is a complex subject and there is much to learn, for example, the importance and the different kinds of omega-3 fatty acids and anti-oxidants. The following are some of the consistent recommendations from the epidemiological, public health, and medical literatures:

- Eat a variety of fruits and vegetables.
- Limit your intake of red meat.
- Make sure you consume adequate amounts of protein.
- Eat nuts, beans, and whole-grain bread.
- Limit your intake of ultra processed foods—those with five or more ingredients or with words that you cannot pronounce. They commonly include: sugary beverages, snack foods, candy, pre-packaged meals, processed meats (hot dogs), breakfast cereals, bakery goods, sauces, fast foods.

If your health plan pays for it (and even if it doesn't) it is helpful to consult a professional dietician occasionally. We recommend that you read *Blue Zones* by Dan Buettner to learn about the benefits of a Mediterranean diet.[2]

314. Sleep. Regardless of whether you are a student or a faculty member, time is an issue—there is never enough of it to do all that needs to be done. When we are busy, this is typically where we steal time from . . . and we are only stealing from ourselves in a very bad way. While you may hear your colleagues brag about how they can get by on four hours of sleep, that is never optimal and very quickly leads to decreased cognitive function, emotional rawness, hormonal imbalance, weight gain, inflammation, and nearly intractable fatigue. Get enough sleep!

315. Who's in charge? You are in charge of your own education and no one will invest in you like you will. So, take care of yourself and listen to your body. When your body is telling you it needs to rest, take time to rest.

316. Meditation. When we suggest meditation, we are not talking about a bearded man sitting cross-legged in front of a cave or high on a mountaintop. You can meditate anywhere, and it's not complicated. Do it for at least ten minutes a day.

Why meditate? The medical literature increasingly highlights the cognitive, physical, and emotional benefits of meditation.

To meditate, simply sit in a quiet room, breathe slowly and deeply, and try not to obsess about your worries or the tasks on your to-do list. To drive such thoughts out of your mind while meditating, you will find it helpful to use a mantra, which is a constantly repeated phrase.

317. Acupuncture. Two of us benefited greatly from acupuncture, one used acupuncture to avoid a complicated surgical procedure. This treatment is not a fad. Chinese medicine, including acupuncture, is about 5,000 years old. Acupuncture is used successfully to treat pain, hypertension, insulin/blood sugar balance, and many other ailments.

We suggest using acupuncture as a complement rather than a replacement for traditional Western medicine. Finding an excellent acupuncture specialist can be challenging, but then finding an excellent cardiologist can also be challenging.

After taking a detailed medical history, the acupuncturist places small needles at just the right spots to combat your ailments as you lie on your back. You will continue to lie there for about 45 minutes once the needles are inserted. Placement of the needles is based on a theory about the flow of vital energy, or *chi*, within your body.

The small needles inserted into your body are quite thin and don't hurt, at least not for the two of us who tried it. However, you may sometimes feel a slight pinching sensation.

318. Physical appearance. How you look and interact is observed continually. Fortunately, you're not expected to come to class dressed in a suit as though you were in a 1930s movie. You are, however, expected by your students and by your colleagues to be neat, with clean and pressed clothes. For young faculty, it helps distinguish you from the students. It also helps if you are thought of as a person who smiles, not frowns.

As you age, your appearance will be affected by your health. For example, as a person involved with books, computers, and student papers, you depend on your vision for your livelihood. It's not shameful for an academic to use glasses (or contacts) rather than squinting. As you head into middle age, you will inevitably become farsighted. Don't do as one colleague we know did and keep pushing menus farther and farther away from your face. Buy some reading glasses (even if you purchase them at the local drugstore).

Hearing is lost a little at a time. For males in particular the high frequencies are the first to go. If you've spent a lot of time at rock concerts or at shooting ranges, your hearing has likely been affected, and the symptoms will show up in class. For example, you might find yourself asking students (particularly those who speak softly) to repeat what they said more loudly "so everyone can hear." What's really going on is that you are having trouble hearing, and you're becoming less effective in class, which sometimes results in poorer teaching ratings. Where hearing aids used to signify your elder age, they have become much more accepted and more easily hidden. They even connect directly to your phone—handy for watching "reels" during boring faculty meetings.

319. Health and life insurance. Most colleges and universities offer health insurance to their full-time faculty as a fringe benefit.[3] It's almost always a better deal than insurance policies you buy on your own. In the first years out of graduate school, you'll need all of the benefits of health insurance a lot less than your older colleagues, and it may seem like a bad deal. Furthermore, in many cases, adding your spouse and kids to your policy will cost you more than your own insurance, sometimes a lot more. If you're married with a working spouse who is also eligible for health insurance, take the coverage from the plan that is lower in cost and better in benefits. However, premiums by themselves are not an indicator of the best plan. For example, different plans involve different copayments you make every time you use the insurance. There are also high deductible plans that might be fine if you are single and healthy . . . and have the deductible stashed away in your savings. Study what is offered and then make a choice. Under no circumstances should you remain without coverage. A serious health disaster can wipe out you and your family financially. Do not ever skimp on health insurance.

Your institution may offer a minimum amount of life insurance at little or no cost. If it's free, certainly take it. If the cost is minimal think hard about it. If you're the main breadwinner or a parent, even a little life insurance will be a great help if you get hit by a car crossing the street.

NOTES

1 According to the *Oxford English Dictionary*, *aero* is from the Greek meaning "air" and *bic* is from the Greek word *bios* meaning "life." The benefits of aerobics include reducing stress, weight control, improved cardiovascular and muscular fitness, increased flexibility, lower cholesterol, and improved sleep patterns.

2 https://www.bluezones.com

3 If you're an adjunct, you probably aren't eligible for health insurance or life insurance. Although you may not be able to get an increase in the pittance that adjuncts are paid because the rates are uniform across the department or the college, you may be able to negotiate some form of health insurance. Try it.

Chapter 16
Final Thoughts

Hint 321 The saying "The rich get richer" holds true in academia as well as in society in general.

FINAL THOUGHTS

This short chapter contains a few final reflections, perspectives, and hints. Despite the practical, even cynical, tone of many of our hints, we, nonetheless, have found that colleges and universities are wonderful places to work. And, as we end the text of this book (with supplemental appendices to follow), we include a bonus hint about an important skill—knowing when to stop working on a project.

320. Work smarter, not harder. There is always an easier way to do things; sometimes it is really hard to figure out.

321. The saying "The rich get richer" holds true in academia as well as in society in general. Once you establish a reputation, people will pursue you to do things, such as write papers, make presentations at prestigious places, and consult. To reach this position you must earn it. If you do reach it, remember that fame is transitory. You must keep running and doing new things to keep up people's demand for you. So, once you become one of the powerful 100 (Hint 2), you will gain rewards, but you will also work furiously to keep your riches. Those who are reading these hints will want to take your place.

322. Treat students as though they were guests in your home. This is simple, sound advice. If you carry nothing else away from these hints, remember this one.

A few final thoughts in this chapter of final thoughts. In these hints we described life based on our own experiences (and mistakes) as well as on observing our colleagues at universities throughout the country. We did not try to quote the many learned studies of academe by academics nor paint a picture of the ideal world that academe *should* be. For example, we believe, as most aspiring academics do, that teaching should be more respected and rewarded than it is, but we know that in many institutions teaching is a necessary, but far from sufficient, condition for tenure.

These hints apply in today's academic job market. We hope the coming demographic reversal will provide the impetus to change the system so this book will be read as an artifact of an ancient, more cynical age.

When we started writing these hints, we found some previous attempts to encapsulate wisdom that is similar to what is found in our book. In typical academician's fashion, of course, we did not read them. We invite readers to send us their own rules, so we may tell future students about them in future editions.

In this book, we are frank, cynical when necessary, and hard-nosed. We provide you with the best career advice we can. We hope this approach does not leave you with a jaundiced view of academia. *We consider being a professor to be the best job available on the planet.* Universities are wonderful, and occasionally transcendent, places to work. Most, but by no means all, of the great intellectual and scientific advances since the Enlightenment were made in universities. It is a thrill and an honor to

Final Thoughts

contribute to knowledge through one's own scholarship. Furthermore, you may well conclude that the most valuable and meaningful work you do is teaching and mentoring students, which is a rare opportunity to guide the expansion and development of young (and older) minds and ideas over your entire lifetime.

Enter this exciting world, but with your eyes wide open. Smile and laugh often. And most importantly, enjoy the journey!

The final hint: It's important to know when to wrap up a project. An obsessive commitment to conducting every possible analysis of your data will delay your project unnecessarily. You can always run additional analyses after your PhD is granted, after your paper is accepted, after. . . . Similarly, endlessly editing and improving your prose yields few benefits and carries significant costs. The perfect project is the enemy of the completed project. The scholars who endlessly rework a paper tend to publish less. Yes, you should carry out thorough and rigorous analyses. Yes, you should edit your paper carefully. But the analysis does not need to be overly complex and the editing does not need to take forever.

Appendices

Appendix A
Mechanics of the Dissertation

We put our thoughts on the mechanics of the dissertation into this appendix because they are of interest for a short but important time: when you are nearing the end of your first draft until you submit the dissertation to the registrar with the requisite payments. They also serve as a reminder for young faculty asked to serve on PhD committees.

323. Oral examinations in the PhD process can occur in at least three points.

- As part of your prelim (or qualifying) examination
- When you present your dissertation proposal to your faculty committee
- When you defend your completed dissertation

You shouldn't go into such meetings without knowing what the structure will be. Ask your dissertation chair what to expect. Part of their role is to ensure that you are properly prepared. In the following, we present a typical pattern for an oral exam. Find out if this template describes how your department structures its meetings.

When you arrive, faculty committee members may ask you to leave the room while they discuss how they want to proceed during the meeting.

After this, you will be asked to give a brief presentation of your written prelims, proposal, or completed dissertation. Carefully plan a clear, well-organized presentation. Keep it brief. Unless your department requires something different, limit your remarks to 10–20 minutes plus time for discussion (questions and answers). Sometimes a faculty member will interrupt you to ask a question. Answer it clearly and fully. The time required to answer usually does not count toward your 10–20 minutes, but find out beforehand if it will.

APPENDIX A

Next, each professor will ask you a series of questions. Answer each to the best of your ability. If you simply don't know an answer, just admit it. Whatever you do, do not try to answer with nonsense filled with buzzword phrases.

Sometimes one professor will jump in while their colleague is questioning you, and the orderly sequence can evaporate. Do not worry if this happens. On rare occasions, two members of your committee will disagree with one another about an issue and start to argue. This is the best of all outcomes from your point of view. Just observe and do not contribute.

When the questioning is completed, you will be asked to leave the room while the faculty members discuss and assess your presentation and responses.

Then they will call you back into the room and give you their feedback.

324. Visual aids in oral presentations. Should you use a visual presentation software like PowerPoint (Hint 113) for your presentation? You have three choices:

- Present your work verbally without a visual aid
- Use PowerPoint
- Distribute printouts of your PowerPoint slides

If your committee requires one mode of presentation, the decision has been made for you. Otherwise, base your choice on your comfort level. Be as calm and focused as possible during this exam. If you feel that PowerPoint will improve your talk and aid your flow, use it. If you panic when a technological glitch occurs, speak without visual aids or distribute hard copies. (Be aware, though, that your committee members may start to read ahead in the copies and tune out your carefully crafted verbal presentation.) Alternatively, you can plan to use PowerPoint but drop it if there is a glitch and distribute the printed version instead.

There is nothing wrong with a simple, clear verbal presentation.

325. Waiting for the committee's decision after the oral examination. It is natural to be anxious while you are standing in the hall or isolated in a zoom room, waiting to learn your committee's decision. Don't panic, even if it takes a long time.

Remember that this occasion may be the first time your faculty committee has met as a group to discuss your work. They will undertake a thoughtful, detailed discussion of your work, its strengths, and areas for improvement. Also, we are sorry to report, sometimes professors stray in these discussions to pressing matters of faculty governance or politics, or to the latest movie, and who knows what else.

326. Post-oral exam rewrites. Usually, the committee requires you to rewrite some of your dissertation after the defense. Don't be surprised, and don't view it as an indication of failure.

The dissertation proposal meeting determines the final shape and design of your dissertation research. Suggested changes can include the research question, how you will proceed, methodology, editorial changes, and additions to the literature review. The faculty believes its recommendation will help you produce a high-quality dissertation. Welcome and incorporate their suggestions—unless you can make a persuasive argument why you should not do so, and they agree. Otherwise, you don't really have a choice.

At the dissertation defense meeting, occasionally you will be asked to conduct an additional analysis. More frequently the faculty will ask for editorial changes. Even if you pass the defense, you have not earned your PhD. You do not finish your graduate studies until you make the changes, and your committee members sign the appropriate approval forms.

Plan for rewriting time after each examination. Do *not* plan to take a trip right after the defense to celebrate or start a new job. If no edits or changes are required, little will be lost. You will have some post-defense breathing room.

327. Faculty signatures. Following each oral examination, faculty members sign the appropriate forms to signify their approval. Because of increased concerns about cybercrime, universities are less likely to ask their professors to place their signatures on a document that will become public. Consequently, signing separate forms often has replaced signing the actual dissertation document.

For prelim orals, the signatures mean you passed.

For a proposal, the signatures mean that your proposal is approved and you are ready to be "advanced to candidacy," with the following three possibilities:

- If no changes are requested, or if the changes are small, the committee members may all sign at the end of the defense.
- If the requested changes are nontrivial, all committee members may wait to sign until the revisions are made.
- In an alternative approach, to streamline the revision process the chair withholds their signature until after your rewrite, but the other committee members sign at the end of the meeting.

Typically, for a dissertation defense, signatures may be collected electronically and may take on a different form, depending on your university. In any case:

- The committee signs stating you have passed the oral defense.
- Each member of the full committee signs that you have successfully completed your dissertation.
- The chair signs that the dissertation is ready for submission. Typically, it is the chair's responsibility to adjudicate any edits requested by the committee.

APPENDIX A

328. External examiners. If you have the option to invite an external examiner or reader to your dissertation defense, carefully weigh the advantages and disadvantages.

This can be an opportunity for you to impress 1 of the 100 powerful people (Hint 2) with the quality of your work, which can lead to a job offer. Conversely, the external reader decides to impress the committee members, or is simply a disagreeable and unpleasant person, and savagely criticizes the student. Because you certainly don't want this situation, find out as much as you can about a distinguished outsider before sending an invitation. Your faculty mentor (Hint 5) can provide useful information and can help by communicating in advance with the outsider.

329. Guests at your dissertation defense. In our age of transparency, your dissertation defense is open to whomever shows up. Fellow graduate students nearing their own defense often come to obtain insight into what the defense is about. Some candidates invite friends and family members to the defense, but we advise against it. Yes, they provided emotional support as you persisted through graduate school, and you would like to share the culmination of your effort with them. But their presence could be awkward for you and for them if the defense takes a critical, or nasty, turn.

330. Submitting your dissertation to the registrar. Your institution's registrar has strict guidelines for the layout of the dissertation you submit, including spacing, margins, table format, and reference specifications, etc. Ask for a style guide and follow those guidelines religiously. Additionally apply them while you are writing your chapters and not at the last minute. They are non-negotiable in the eyes of the registrar.

Appendix B
Outside Income

Professors, being human, want to maximize their income no matter how large or small it is. Opportunities exist for earning more from the university through teaching overloads, summer sessions, or executive or noncredit courses, among others. However, most schools treat you for such work the same way they treat adjunct faculty. They pay as little as possible to maximize their income.

This appendix discusses outside income from consulting, grants, and contracts. In Appendix C, we'll talk about other sources of income such as writing textbooks (Hint 162) or serving as an expert witness (Hint 297).

331. Consulting as a hired hand. Consulting involves doing work for an organization for compensation, as opposed to your professional activities that contribute to your field but are not compensated. Examples of professional activities include reviewing papers submitted to journals, reviewing grant proposals, and serving on or chairing committees of a national or local professional association. In consulting, you are a hired hand, asked to give advice about what to do, typically paid on a time basis.

332. Don't live on your consulting income. Consulting income is found money; it comes to you episodically. Do not plan on future consulting income under any circumstances when constructing your family budget. Even if you can trace a steady $5,000 or more per year from consulting over the past six years, you are not guaranteed to earn any consulting income next year unless you have a contract in hand. Even then, corporate fortunes change, and you can be terminated. We recommend you use your consulting income after you receive it to buy large, durable items (a new TV or computer or refrigerator) or save it for a major vacation or to buy a house.

Remember, as a consultant you are running a business, and one of the risks is that you, like a plumber or a painter, don't always get paid what you and your client agreed on.

333. Consulting income is taxable. Don't go out and spend the consulting checks you receive until you have put money aside to pay the taxes on it. Consulting income is like all other income and can put you into a higher tax bracket. Whoever hires you as a consultant will file a 1099 form, and the Internal Revenue Service (IRS) is superb at using that form to find you if you don't report the income. Fortunately, you report your consulting income on a special form (Schedule C) which allows you to deduct legitimate expenses incurred in generating the income. We strongly recommend you consult a tax specialist about how to prepare a Schedule C. A good tax specialist who knows what can and cannot be deducted will often save you a considerable amount of money and is worth the investment.

334. Grants and contracts. Receiving an academic salary for nine months' work seems to leave you vast amounts of time to undertake lucrative additional work, such as consulting. It usually does not work out that way because your teaching responsibilities often spill over into summer. More to the point, even if you are a full professor, you may need that summer for research and writing. The best way to earn extra income while moving toward academic goals is to secure grants and contracts. Most federal agencies and other funding organizations that provide research support for summer work usually pay the equivalent of two months' salary (i.e., two ninths of your academic salary). Some may provide three months' support. Some, but not all, research universities allow faculty to work one day a week during the regular year for pay by outside sources.

335. The summer teaching option. Junior and senior professors sometimes slip into doing extensive summer teaching, usually at reduced rates. It is a way of earning needed extra income by doing something you know how to do. You should know that you incur what the economists call an *opportunity cost* associated with this income, meaning you close off other opportunities, especially those in research and writing that could advance your career. However, if your school offers substantial summer research grants, go for them.

336. Regular income versus Schedule C income. Payment you receive through your school (such as summer pay) is usually considered regular income. You may not be able to use Schedule C to report it or to deduct the associated expenses.

337. Pro bono work. If you are a beginning professor, chances are you are struggling to make ends meet. Whenever you can seize the opportunity, you should consider doing some consulting jobs pro bono, that is, for free. Each of us have taken on a number of "jobs" pro bono. Our pro bono work has led to fantastic paid opportunities—don't snub your nose at it. In addition, even when pro bono work does not lead to a consulting opportunity, you are using your expertise to make a contribution to society.

338. Consulting pay rate. If you are being considered for a consulting job, you will be asked what your consulting rate is. Fees for consulting vary by discipline and by client, Therefore, it is difficult for us to suggest generic rules that always work. Nonetheless, here is a best practice guideline for your daily rate for business clients:

- Take the annual pay in your nine-month contract and divide it by 165, the standard number of working days in nine months. That calculation gives your daily income from your institution.
- Multiply the number you just computed by 2, because you must be paid more for your knowledge than just your regular pay, and it also takes care of deductions such as Social Security and Medicare taxes.

For example, if your nine-month salary is $66,000, dividing that by 165 yields a daily income of $400. Multiplying $400 by 2 results in $800/day (or $100/hour) as your consulting rate.

Some additional considerations:

- Charge nonprofit organizations a lower rate than for-profit groups. They have less money and usually are not able to afford your full rate.
- If you are really a world expert in your field, or if your school's salaries are in the lower quartile of academic salaries, you can of course charge more than the amount computed in the method above.
- If you can, find out what other consultants are charging the firm. It's a delicate question to ask, and some people will inflate their actual rate. Nonetheless, don't be bashful about it. If you ask too much, you lose a client; if you ask too little, you'll kick yourself for it later.
- Should you charge for travel time in addition to travel cost reimbursement? Sometimes you must travel quite a distance to the organization or company that hired you. It is better to address this issue explicitly when you are negotiating the consulting agreement. We tend not to charge for travel time (but do charge for travel expenses) if we are not working on the client's project while traveling. Some consultants charge half their rate for travel time.

339. Warning! Teaching elsewhere may be a conflict of interest. Universities and colleges do not let you moonlight at another school without permission. It's a conflict of interest. The specific permission rules vary from place to place, but every institution has them. We know of one case where a tenured faculty member in an eastern US university took a second appointment in another university within driving distance. When found out, he was asked to resign by both, and he had to.

Appendix C
How to Become a Millionaire

In this appendix we discuss several strategies that could make you wealthy, since your university salary only goes so far. Achieving wealth with these strategies is quite rare. Unlike all the other hints in this book, they are likely to *damage*, if not *destroy,* your academic career rather than improve it.

This appendix is largely tongue-in-cheek. It's a long shot, but you can become wealthy as an academic. For example, a specialist in operations research, a tenured full professor, developed a successful system to beat racehorses. He gave advice on the racing form as "Dr. Z."[1] We have worked with academic researchers who were billionaires, but they earned their money the old-fashioned way—they inherited it. Most of us, however, chose academia because we are motivated by other goals and values.

340. Making (or not making) a fortune through publishing and public appearances. As a professor, you have (or can create) opportunities for making money beyond your university or college pay. While some people will clamor for your services, other times you need to go out and solicit opportunities. Here are some opportunities categorized by their potentially (but not certain) large payoffs:

- Writing textbooks (see Hint 162), but pay attention to the caveats in the hints
- Writing popular nonfiction (e.g., history, public policy) or fiction
- Performing in public (if you are a musician, singer, actor, or lecturer)
- Consulting in industry or government
- Owning or running a business on the side (be careful that it is not a perceived conflict of interest—perception can be reality)
- Being a professional expert witness

Opportunities that almost certainly have small payoffs are:

- Writing op-ed pieces for newspapers
- Serving as a proposal reviewer for government research agencies or book publishers
- Honoraria, such as for editing a journal
- Appearing on television as an expert
- Writing books, such as the one you're reading, for small audiences

Be aware, however, that these opportunities take away some of your valuable time professionally and personally. They don't help you achieve tenure or promotion, and they can generate jealousies that affect your career negatively (Hint 162). If the payoff proves to be small, you will often wind up working for less than minimum wage. On the other hand, if you rake in enough, you can quit your job and live off the profits. Regardless, they can be fun—like writing this book.

341. Write a best-selling novel. Consider Erich Segal. He was launched on a promising academic career as a tenure-track professor in classics at Yale. He came to Yale with bachelor's (with honors), master's, and PhD degrees from Harvard where he served as class poet and Latin orator.

In 1970 he wrote a romantic novel, *Love Story,* set at Harvard. This book was an enormous best seller, although the critics did not consider it great literature. One wrote, "it skips from cliche to cliche with an abandon that would chill even the blood of a True Romance editor."[2] Nonetheless, there were 21 printings in the first 12 months, and the initial paperback printing was 4.3 million copies.[3] He wrote the screenplay for the movie, which grossed $200 million and was credited with saving Paramount Studios from bankruptcy. Segal became an international celebrity and later worked with John Lennon on the screenplay for *Yellow Submarine.*

Segal was subsequently denied tenure at Yale.

Moral: Don't make your tenure reviewers jealous.

342. Use a pseudonym for non-academic publications. If you are convinced your novel will be a blockbuster, consider using a pseudonym. For example, the late Carolyn Gold Heilbrun was the Avalon Foundation Professor in the humanities and the first woman tenured in the Columbia University English Department. She published a number of highly regarded academic books, but she also published a successful series of novels as Amanda Cross.

Pseudonyms are frequently employed by professionals whose writing might conflict with the norms or expectations of their day jobs.

APPENDIX C

343. Start your own consulting firm. Once you have your degree, consider expanding your consulting activities by launching a consulting firm. If the firm is successful and grows, you may find yourself running a multimillion-dollar organization. Needless to say, you need professional knowledge of your consulting discipline, salesmanship, proposal writing skills, management expertise, and a good deal of luck.

There are many very successful and profitable consulting firms started by those in academia that go on to outlive their founders.

344. Write a college textbook. It's possible to become wealthy by writing a textbook. If you produce a good, clear textbook, especially for a course offered in most colleges and universities, the royalties are substantial, especially if new students will be taking that course year after year.

However, there are some drawbacks:

- It will probably damage your academic career, although there are exceptions. Paul Samuelson and Paul Krugman each won the Nobel Prize in Economics and wrote leading introductory economics textbooks.
- Other people will have had the same idea; the competition is considerable.
- In rapidly changing fields, your book will quickly become outdated. In slowly changing fields, you will need to revise your textbook from time to time.
- Writing a textbook usually is like teaching an introductory course. You are not building greater knowledge or a greater reputation in your specialty.

Sometimes publishers take a chance on your book if you can guarantee sales in your own courses over the next three or four years. With luck, the book will take off and become a standard.

345. Write a textbook for K-12 education. If successful, a K-12 text could be more lucrative than winning the lottery. In many states, textbooks are adopted for all students in a given grade. Should your book be adopted by a state, hopefully a populous one, the guaranteed sales are enormous.

However, you are entering a world of complex, byzantine maneuvering and competition. Major textbook publishers are powerful, and for minor publishers it's tough sledding competing with them.

346. Write a crossover book. Professors build their reputations by publishing articles and books in their specialties. Almost always, their only readers are other professors, graduate students, and their own families. Sometimes, however, a faculty member produces a successful crossover book, a work that is respected and receives laudatory reviews from their academic colleagues while also selling well with the general public.

Such books are difficult to write, however. If your book is to fly off the proverbial shelves at Amazon, it has to be readable and entertaining. Few people reach the level of clear and creative writing that is required for that. Furthermore, even among highly skilled professional nonfiction writers, New York Times best sellers are rare.

Nonetheless, some university scholars have written best sellers, including Peter Drucker, Margaret Mead, Paul Krugman, Gail Kearns Goodwin, and Stephen Hawking.

We believe that professors who produce crossover books perform a valuable public service. However, remember Hint 162: Unless you become a world-class public intellectual like the people in the preceding paragraph, you may be denigrated by your academic peers as a mere popularizer. A false equation that does not work mathematically but still describes the behavior of many misguided professors is excellent technical productivity plus commercial success is respected less than excellent technical productivity alone.

347. Save by using a TIAA or other annuity plan. If you are risk averse (Hint 86 and 212), you will likely judge each of the previous approaches to be too dependent on luck for you to attempt. The recession that started in 2007 highlighted the risk of speculating in stocks or bonds. A really risk-averse person should consider the retirement plan offered by their institution to determine whether the result is a million-dollar nest egg. When combined with Social Security, the result could be a payout of about $100,000 per year before taxes.

If your institution belongs to TIAA, which is the portable 403(b) retirement plan offered by most colleges and universities, you can wind up accumulating the million in cash from the combination of your employer's and your own tax-deferred contributions.

Corollary: Many of the retirement systems for state universities and colleges guarantee an annuity based on your three highest years of salary. These annuities can also create large annual payouts.

Bottom line: If you plan to stay in academia, you can become a millionaire through an annuity, but you have to wait until retirement to cash in.

NOTES

1 He noticed that the odds displayed at the track were based only on win bets; place and show bets often followed a different pattern. Income was made in this discrepancy.

D. B. Hausch, W. T. Ziemba, M. Rubinstein (1981) "Efficiency of the market for racetrack betting." *Management Science* 27(12): 1435–1452.

2 https://erichsegal.com. Accessed August 11, 2024.

3 https://www.latimes.com/archives/la-xpm-2010-jan-20-la-me-erich-segal20-2010jan20-story.html. Accessed August 11, 2024.

Appendix D
Writing Hints

This appendix expands on Chapter 7: On Writing. It contains tips that will help you in writing and editing your manuscripts, whether they are your dissertation, papers, books, or monographs. These tips are based on our experiences. Furthermore, one of us spent eight years as a technical editor. Good, logical, readable writing increases the odds that your submission will be accepted.

We use the term "paper" in what follows to represent all forms of publication. You may find that specific journals and publishers have idiosyncrasies of their own. If so, follow them rather than us.

348. Explain only what the reader needs to know. Don't try to explain your field or subfield from first principles. You are not writing a textbook for undergraduates or an article for your alumni magazine. You can assume that your reader is familiar with the field in general and knows all that. Do explain what readers need to know for them to understand what you are saying.

349. Avoid passive voice, which is dull and pedantic. Typically, in passive voice, you use the verb first and then the subject. Active voice makes your work interesting to read. In active voice, the subject performs the action given in the verb, such as in the following:

Passive voice: The girl was bitten by the dog.

Active voice: The dog bit the girl.

Passive voice: Statistical tests were conducted to check the validity of the hypothesis.

Active voice: Statistical tests checked the validity of the hypothesis.

350. Avoid "should" and "must." These prescriptive words assume you are in a position to give advice and that you found the only way to do something, which is rarely the case. Authors of business and policy papers are particularly fond of this bad habit, although it also shows up in many other fields. As we, the authors, are only human, please ignore our use of them in this book.

351. Pay attention to fonts. All caps is accepted as yelling at someone—do not do it. Use bold, italics, and underline sparingly for emphasis or as a call out of something important.

352. You can rarely be *effective and efficient.* Some people use these words together almost as if they were a single word. It is rare to achieve both simultaneously; usually the best you can do is trade one for the other. If you are using them together, ensure that you are truly effective *and* efficient.

353. Avoid generalizing from a single case. You are limited to the results from that case and that case alone. It is generally accepted that cases are not generalizable and that they illustrate the art of the possible.

354. Don't be afraid to use numbered or bulleted lists. Don't try to put everything into straight text, otherwise you might wind up writing something that looks like:

A method . . .

Another method . . .

Another method . . .

A fourth method . . .

It is better to say:

The methods are the following:

1. . . .
2. . . .
3. . . .
4. . . .

Because a list breaks material up visually, it helps your reader follow you more easily.

355. Use figures and tables. Like lists, figures and tables break up the monotony of text. They make information easier to read and understand. Most word processing programs include functions that let you create tables and draw simple figures.

356. Learn to use styles in word processing programs. Microsoft Word and most other text programs contain features that make it easy to create different-looking documents. The journal you write a paper for or the book publisher will specify what format they want for submissions. Styles, built into the word processor, let you change the appearance of the document automatically to fit your requirements. Keep in mind that many publishers will want you to submit your final paper without any hidden formatting, of which styles is one, as is your software-created reference list at the end of your paper.

357. Use the spell-checker. Papers with spelling errors are often rejected out of hand. At the least they show that you are either careless or illiterate, neither of which are desirable traits. Use your software's spell-checker on the final draft. Be careful, however. Often, you can misspell a word and the spell-checker accepts it. For example, if you type "their" when you meant to type "there," the spell-checker won't show it as an error. Spell-check might also correct a word to a wrong, sometimes embarrassing word.

After running the spell-checker and making corrections, be sure to read the paper one more time from end to end (better still, ask someone else to read it as well) before you send it out.

358. Pay special attention to references. Your paper's reviewers and your readers will read your in-text citations and turn to the list of references. Use the following tips:

- Be sure your references are accurate in name spellings, dates of publication, journal name or publisher, and other details. Remember, an author of one of your references may review your paper. Think about the retribution if you spell the author's name wrong.
- Provide a source for all quoted matter. If you quote someone or some source, be sure to include a reference with full publishing information. If you don't, you can be accused of plagiarism.
- Use multiple references when you synthesize several sources. Be sure to include references for all the sources you use.
- Be sure each URL has a date. If you can't find an author's name, use the title in its place. (Use n.d. [no date] if a date is not available.) Depending

on your reference style, you may be asked for the access date. If you always indicate it in your bibliography manager software, then it will always be there, regardless of the reference style used.
- Compile a list of references at the end of your paper.

Exception 1: Some journals require references in footnotes.
Exception 2: Book publishers sometimes use references in chapter endnotes.
When using an in-text citation, follow the style requirements of the journal or book publisher, for example: "The results (Smith 1998; Smith and Jones 2004) . . . "; and "As shown by Jones (2006) . . . " Refer to one of several references by the same author in the same year by adding a, b, c, and so on to the year (Smith, 2004b).

359. Eliminate poor writing habits, for example:

- Avoid "there are" particularly at the start of a sentence.
  - Replace: There are three ways to obtain knowledge, . . .
  - With: Three ways to obtain knowledge are . . .
- Don't split infinitives by putting one or more words between *to* and the verb. You can always write your way around a split infinitive.
  - Replace: To successfully manage knowledge, . . .
  - With: To manage knowledge successfully, . . .
- Do not use "etc." The reader does not know what you include in your *et cetera*. Readers often interpret etc. differently from you. You can convey the same idea by using "including" or "such as."
  - Replace: text, voice, graphics, etc.
  - With: including text, voice, and graphics
- Use "to" instead of "in order to." In most cases, particularly at the beginning of paragraphs, "to" is sufficient. You need "in order to" only when you mean "for the purpose of."
  - Replace: In order to obtain knowledge, . . .
  - With: To obtain knowledge, . . .

360. Bad words refers to words that cause the reader difficulty rather than words banned by the Federal Communications Commission. Words listed in the first column of Table D.1 are best avoided. The second column explains why. The words are representative. In general, if a word is a cliché or hyperbole or advertising or pretentious, replace it with a simpler word that conveys your meaning.

APPENDIX D

Table D.1 Bad Words

Word(s) to Avoid	Reason
Cutting-edge	Cliché
Comprise	*Comprise* is used correctly when you say the whole comprises, or is *comprised of*, the parts (e.g., The Union comprises 50 states), but incorrectly if you say the parts comprise the whole (e.g., Fifty states constitute [or *make up* or *compose*] the Union, rather than *comprise* it).
Discovered	Usually you mean to say *found* or *obtained*. Discovery implies scientific discovery, or when the known world was smaller, finding a previously unknown territory.
Dramatically	It's meaningless hyperbole. Do you mean a Noh play in which little happens, or a melodrama?
Finally	Not needed at the beginning of a sentence or as the last item in a list. The reader can tell from the context that it is the end.
Ideal	*Ideal* means "absolute perfection" and is unprovable.
Incredible	Hyperbole
It is important	Let the reader find out that something is important.
Perfect	Hyperbole. You can rarely prove perfection.
Perfect solution	Advertising hyperbole
Recent	Academic writing is read for many years after publication. Something published in 2007 is recent in 2008 but not in 2012.
This	When used alone, the antecedent of "this" is not clear. For example, "This proves the hypothesis" should be replaced by "This analysis proves the hypothesis."
Utilize	*Utilize* is not a synonym for the verb "use." *Utilize* means "to make use of" and sounds pretentious.

For Product Safety Concerns and Information please contact our EU representative GPSR@taylorandfrancis.com
Taylor & Francis Verlag GmbH, Kaufingerstraße 24, 80331 München, Germany

www.ingramcontent.com/pod-product-compliance
Lightning Source LLC
Chambersburg PA
CBHW052020290426
44112CB00014B/2313